IN PURSUIT OF ECSTASY

By the same author

In Pursuit of Infidelity

IN PURSUIT OF ECSTASY

Sujata Parashar

RUPA

Copyright © Sujata Parashar 2011

Published by
Rupa Publications India Pvt. Ltd.
7/16, Ansari Road, Daryaganj,
New Delhi 110 002

Sales Centres:
Allahabad Bengaluru Chennai
Hyderabad Jaipur Kathmandu
Kolkata Mumbai

All rights reserved.
No part of this publication may be reproduced, stored in a
retrieval system, or transmitted, in any form or by any means,
electronic, mechanical, photocopying, recording or otherwise,
without the prior permission of the publishers.

The author asserts the moral right to be identified
as the author of this work.

Printed at Repro Knowledgecast Limited, Thane

CONTENTS

Author's Note	*vii*
Acknowledgements	*ix*
Principal Characters	*xi*
Prologue	*xiii*
Aparajita	1
Deepanita	33
Aniket	53
Siddharth	63
Ritesh and Sushanto	71
The Twin Announcements	91
The Game Plan	103
Trip to Shimla	135
Back in Kolkata	187
Destination Delhi	213
Epilogue	225

AUTHOR'S NOTE

This book has been inspired by today's youth and their outlook towards life. Let us nurture our children in a free and caring environment without putting the burden of our own expectations and aspirations on their young shoulders and teach them just one thing – To be Happy!

Let us appreciate our parents and the hidden agenda behind their constant 'Do's and Don'ts' – to see their children prosper and be happy in life.

> ". . . *The last time the National Crime Record Bureau (NCRB) updated its record in 2007, it found that two out of five individuals (41.3%) arrested in India belonged to the 18 – 30 age group . . .*"
>
> – *Outlook*, November 16, 2009

ACKNOWLEDGEMENTS

All the people in the list have helped me immensely and unconditionally.

Anjana Kher (my confidant and guide)

Yashwant Deval (an ever resourceful friend)

Raheel Anwar (a dad who himself proclaims albeit jokingly, that his kids don't listen to him any more)

Sumeet Panigarhi (a talented writer who gave me some very useful inputs for the book)

Nav Qirti (the best networked person I have known besides being my husband)

Col S.K. Parashar (my father and mentor)

Simriti Parashar (my loving mother)

Ashish Sharma (my ever encouraging Mausaji)

A very important resource person (who refused to be named but without whose correct inputs it might have been difficult to complete this book – and so it would be unjustified if I do not mention him and express my heartfelt thanks here).

All the youngsters (I interacted with and observed during the time I wrote this book).

My publisher, editor and rest of the team at Rupa, whom I completely admire for their fair and positive outlook, dedication and professionalism.

Last, but not the least my son Lokevidu – who needless to say makes me a proud and happy person!

PRINCIPAL CHARACTERS

Youth	Father/ Guardian	Mother	Sibling(s)
Aparajita	Neel Mukherjee	Brinda Mukherjee	–
Deepanita	Bhaskar Ganguly	Shrishti Ganguly	Girish, Partho
Siddharth	Kalyan Banerjee	Ritu Banerjee	–
Aniket	Joydeep Choudhary	Nishi Choudhary	–
Ritesh	Mamu	–	Sushanto Mishra

PROLOGUE

January 2009

'Order! Order! Please maintain courtroom decorum!' boomed the grim-looking judge. The room was filled with some of the most distinguished faces of the country. The trial was coming to an end. Many of the faces tried to keep in check their worst-known fears. But with the verdict drawing to a close, they could not control it anymore and broke into panicky murmurs. They tried to draw their own verbal conclusions and at the same time pacify the others.

Unfazed by all this, Siddharth looked at the girl he loved and wanted to protect. She was crying inconsolably and the frenzied media was capturing all of it in their heartless cameras. He wanted to break their machines but was helpless. His hands were handcuffed. His eyes sought hers…and after some painful moments of trying to catch her attention he gave up. But just then, as if sensing his need, she looked up at him through her tear-stricken face. She looked even more innocent and beautiful than he had known. And then, before his eyes could tell her what his heart wanted to, she quickly looked away. She seemed really ashamed of herself. He blamed himself for that look.

I wish I could tell her… how much I love her. And that everything will be all right. No one can harm her. I will not let anyone hurt her ever again. That bloody…! He checked his emotions as he knew it was of no use now. The damage had been done. The guilty will be punished but the innocent will bear the scar, Siddharth thought to himself sadly. Then his eyes fell on the other girl and the bespectacled boy who according to him were actually responsible for the present situation. Not wanting to dwell on it, his eyes searched the courtroom for his 'once proud' parents. He found them sitting in the middle of the second row looking equally dejected, worried and melancholic. He recognised the other parents sitting in the same row along with them. They too, had the same expression as the one in his parents' eyes.

'Under the Narcotics Drugs and Psychotropic Substances Act, Mr Sushanto Mishra and Mr Ritesh Mishra are found guilty of possessing and being involved in trafficking of dangerous narcotics. They are sentenced to ten years of rigorous imprisonment and a fine of ₹3 lakhs each. Their associate Mr K. Chabra also found equally guilty for the same crime will be sentenced to ten years of rigorous imprisonment and a fine of ₹3 lakhs. Convicts were involved in the trafficking and selling of Cocaine and Ecstasy – two very dangerous drugs.' He said gravely.

'…illegal trade of the same in such huge quantities could have had an adverse impact on the lives of many young persons as was witnessed by the parents of all the youngsters caught during the police raid…at the so called *"rave party"*. Some of the youths caught during the raid were let off with a fair warning, except….' The judge looked up and repeated '…except the four students of Presidency College, Kolkata – Aparajita Mukherjee,

Deepanita Ganguly, Aniket Choudhary and Siddharth Banerjee who are declared offenders....' The judge went on and on....

But Siddharth, like the others had stopped listening. They were all lost in the past. The recent past which never for once made them suspect or fear the consequences of their actions. If they had had an inkling about the public humiliation, pain and the highly possible jail term that they would have to encounter due to their careless attitudes...maybe they would have refrained from lying and would have kept the elders 'in the know of things' from the very beginning.

August 2008 - Kolkata

APARAJITA

1

The morning rays played hide-and-seek with her freshly shampooed shoulder-length hair, as Aparajita bent down to have the last morsel of the *paurotha* (Indian pan-fried bread). Her mother insisted she have it everyday before leaving for college.

'Mom I am done. Leaving for college now,' Aparajita informed her mother, preoccupied with the morning newspaper and at the same time absent-mindedly nibbling the almost untouched *aloo bhaja* (fried potatoes).

'But *beta* you haven't finished your breakfast yet....' Her mother, a tall and pleasant looking lady with longer (braided) hair than her daughter's and a definite head turner in her own right, said in a loud cajoling voice from their large sun-lit kitchen, which was a part of their ancestral bungalow.

Aparajita looked at her plate and made a comical face of a daughter unwillingly doing a favour to her mother. She replied back, 'Mom, I am already late. Besides, I cannot eat *paurothas* everyday. You are bent upon making me fat!'

On hearing her daughter's reply, her mother called out again, addressing her nineteen-year-old with her pet-name, 'Aupora…Now…now wait for a while, I am making you another one. Eat it and then leave.' Her mother ordered in an authoritative voice.

After a brief moment's pause, she continued, 'And no one in their wildest dream can call you fat. You are hardly visible.'

Before mom can blackmail me into eating a second paurotha *with her favourite* aloo bhaja *(fried potatoes), I should run.*

And instead of answering back she hurriedly got up from the chair and fled, only stopping for a second to pick up her notebooks from the large living-room table.

Aparajita's father, Mr Neel Mukherjee a promising politician had inherited the bungalow from his father who belonged to a well-respected old Zamindar family of Kolkata and was himself quite well known as a great academician during his time. Although, after inheriting it from his father, Mr Mukherjee had revamped the whole place as per his wife, Brinda's wishes and modern-day living requirements. It was ensured that the bungalow maintain its original British era architectural design, including the mosaic flooring and the old yet beautiful, sturdy furniture and a few priceless pieces of paintings. The bungalow was famously called 'Lal Bari' due to its brick-red colour. Over the years it had become a landmark for the people around the posh residential area of College Street.

'Oke dhaur oke dhaur (Go catch her)...' her mother instructed her ever loyal, widowed maid, Kobita urgently in Bengali, on hearing her daughter's quick receding steps. Kobita made it look as if she had hurriedly gone after her employer's daughter, but actually gave Aparajita enough time to flee.

She had been with the family ever since Aparajita was born. And now, after nineteen years, she had become an integral part of the family. Aparajita along with her few close friends who came to her house (after a careful screening by Aparajita herself), lovingly called her Pishi Ma (Aunt).

'She has already left,' replied the dusky, middle-aged maid in Bengali as she returned to the kitchen, a ghost of a smile lighting up her doting eyes at the thought that she was able to help the mischievous teenager whom she loved as her own daughter.

2

I am going to be late for my Economics class. Aparajita thought to herself nervously, as she impatiently waited for her regular auto-rickshaw to drop her to college.

Prof Bose is quite good to me, unlike his reputation of being a very strict professor. But he sure is a stickler for punctuality. I am sure he will understand this once. She tried to put her restless mind to rest.

After all, having a politician for a father and a social activist for a mother had its advantages. She went on thinking, an unconscious mischievous smile playing on her lips. She sat in the auto and Bholu, its owner smiled at her indulgently. Aparajita smiled back widely.

Even though she had a car at her disposal she preferred the auto-rickshaw. And she was glad to know that her parents had not opposed her when she had mentioned this fact to them. In fact they approved of her simple-living and high-thinking actions.

'*Kaimon aacho Dada?* (How are you brother?)' Aparajita asked Bholu, once she settled down on the hard and the bit slippery seat of the auto-rickshaw.

'Aaiye je chole jachee (Just carrying on with life)…' Bholu replied and smiled at the beautiful girl he had seen growing up in front of him.

God is certainly kind to certain people, he thought to himself as he geared up the auto. Take for example, this kind soul sitting in my rickshaw…she is not only gorgeous; but also the only daughter of one of the richest and most powerful men in the city. Of course, he is also a man of compassion and principle and has won many hearts including mine. It was solely because of him that I had been able to easily repay the loan for my auto-rickshaw on time and save my only means of livelihood. Bholu reminded himself of his benefactor's kindness and timely help with a feeling of gratitude towards him.

'Dada…please hurry up…I am already late by five minutes today. Prof Bose will kill me….' The anxious voice of Aparajita broke into his thoughts.

'Ha ha ha…,' Bholu laughed throatily at the worried tone he was habituated to listening almost every other day and said *'achha achha…'* He started manoeuvring his auto expertly through the narrow lanes of College Street, already crowded with noisy pedestrians, honking rickshaws and other vehicles trying to beat one another.

Even though they reached her college through the narrow short-cut quite well known to her, she was already late by seventeen minutes.

'Dada, keep the change.' Aparajita hurriedly handed over the money to Bholu and ran through the college gate.

Once inside, she slowed down her steps to look at the elegant and tall college building of Presidency College with pride. It was one of the oldest and most reputed colleges of Kolkata and its

In Pursuit of Ecstasy • 7

alumni list boasted of some of the most famous personalities of the city and country. Aparajita was proud to be its student.

The corner building meant for arts and entertainment activities reminded Aparajita of something and her flawless pretty face broke into an unconscious smile again. *Oh wow… we have our dance practice after college today! I had almost forgotten that in my rush. It is going to be so much fun. I wonder if Deepanita remembered to get my ghungroos (anklets) today? She is so forgetful. I hope she does, otherwise I will take hers…that will teach her a lesson not to forget it the next time.* Aparajita answered her own question decisively.

After all, it is her fault that I have not been able to practise with them for the past two classes. She justified her stance as she walked hurriedly towards her classroom. *Oh…how I wish I could take a pair of them home and practise in front of my mirror. But it can't be!* Her thoughts suddenly became melancholic as she unwillingly thought about her past.

She could distinctly picture the day when her otherwise 'almost always' busy father decided to call his daughter to his room and chat with her about her progress. 'Think of it *beti*…,' her father went on dreamily while she sat quietly listening to him, next to the old, large, four-poster bed on which he was resting, '…as a competent and reputed statistician or economist who would be able to predict important figures for the State and the country you will make us all so proud of you. You will be in the front pages of all the national dailies with the headlines 'The next Amartya Sen – Ms Aparajita Mukherjee, daughter of the well-known politician Mr Neel Mukherjee.' How proud will I feel that day? You will make me proud won't you Aupora…?' He looked back at his only daughter expecting and wanting nothing less than full compliance to his wishes and dreams. Unable to voice her defiance, she had just silently nodded her head.

But these conversations had left her feeling burdened and depressed. Being the only daughter, she could never openly contradict him and tell him that she did not want to predict boring figures or find out male/female ratios.

'Ma, I want to be a choreographer...and spread joy among as many people as I can by becoming a professional dance composer.' She would instead try and reason out with her mother. To her, dancing was more meaningful and exciting than predicting numbers. But her mother never responded to her excited pleas. She chose to either smile away or keep silent on the topic. Aparajita understood her body language but never really took her mother's silence as 'No' for an answer.

Instead, she managed to keep her parents satisfied by her above-average performance in studies. Aparajita would participate and represent her college in debate competitions, win top prizes and equally excel in sports too, all this, made her quite popular. She would enjoy these activities, but her heart was in dance. And becoming an economist was something she even remotely did not wish to become. *How will I be able to tell my parents about my career plans when the time finally comes?* This question would continuously haunt her.

3

'So what kept you Aparajita...?' Prof Bose who had already seen her coming through the large classroom window, asked her as soon as she was at the door. He looked at her sternly, waiting for an explanation.

For a moment she looked nonplussed. She was so busy with her own thoughts that she failed to prepare herself for her confrontation with the professor.

'Uh...huh...Sir my apologies...actually entirely my mother's doing.' She said the first thing that came to her mind.

Inside she cursed herself for not being prepared for the obvious question and acting so dumb. It is going to be tough. *Think...think...think hard.* She scolded herself.

Aparajita was used to lying. In fact some of her close friends swore that she was the best liar they had known in their lives. The lies would just tumble out genuinely from her mouth like she was telling 'the truth' and 'nothing but the truth'. But with Prof Bose it was the first time and she was understandably nervous.

'Well, don't stand there like a stupid child, explain yourself.' The short heighted Professor looked up at her and boomed impatiently.

'Sir...actually my mother had to go to a seminar organised for the school-dropout, adolescent girls on 'the importance of education for a girl child'. She coaxed me into joining her so that I could interact with the girls and share my views on education and why it is so important for a better living.' She said, meeting his gaze directly and secretly proud of her skills.

'...and she also said that being from the same peer group I would have an impact on them. I would have not gone, but she promised me that I would be back on time to attend my classes.' Aparajita paused for air and the professor's reaction. She got no response but continued.

'…errrr…you see sir, some people were late for the seminar and everything got delayed. I am sorry sir. Next time, I will not go with her even if she insists.' Aparajita ended looking solemn, apologetic and completely sure of herself.

She knew that the name of either of her parents usually made her case stronger and so she would use them when she had to add weight to her cock-and-bull story. (Though, she rarely used their names lest someone checked back with them.) But this time she was sure that even though her mother's name had tumbled out of her mouth before she could think of anything else, it would definitely put her in a better light and make a foolproof case for her with her Economics professor, Mr Bose would never check back. It was beneath his prestige, besides her excuse was leak proof.

'Hmmm…what your mother did was absolutely right. Our girls must study if we want to prosper as a nation.' The professor concluded, and his stern voice softened.

'If a girl is educated she will know its value and will make sure that her own children get proper education too. So you did a good thing by listening to your mother and going with her.' The visibly pleased professor, himself a parent to two bright teenaged girls, informed the 'by now completely confident' Aparajita. Though he was talking to her he looked at the rest of the class as if telling them to follow her example of social service.

Deepanita winked at her as soon as Aparajita occupied the seat next to her. She was sure that her best friend had lied through her teeth to Prof Bose. Deepanita knew her friend well. Even Kobita Pishi did not know so much about her as Deepanita did. They were neighbours and had practically grown up together, had gone to the same school and joined the same college to be close to each other. In fact, it was Deepanita who had introduced her to the magical world of dancing.

Physically and characteristically both were opposites yet they were the thickest of friends. Deepanita was short and slightly on the plump side. But her shoulder-length soft curly hair, oval face, spectacled twinkling eyes made her look very delicate and feminine. With her warm smile, she was considered pretty and the sensible kinds by many. However, Aparajita, with her tall, shapely figure, expressive dark kohled eyes, long silky hair, smooth dusky skin and a prettily pierced nose, was the much admired one. Also because of her penchant for discussions, debates and outdoor sports, she was liked by girls and boys alike.

'So you managed to hoodwink Mr 'fool me not',' Deepanita whispered to her friend, suppressing a smile. They used to call Prof Bose that name as his favourite dialogue was 'you people cannot fool me...'

'Yeah just got saved by my skin today...all thanks to my hidden art,' Aparajita replied feeling mischievous and guilty at the same time. Both the girls started to giggle but suppressed it quickly lest the sharp-eyed professor caught them both laughing in his class.

4

The next period was History and since both of them had opted out of it, they were free to pass their time frivolously till the next class. They decided to head for the college canteen for their usual cup of coffee.

'Dada please make us two strong coffees and a plate of *aaloor chop* (deep-fried potato rolls)'. Deepanita ordered for both of them.

The famous Bengali snack was Deepanita's favourite. And though Aparajita was openly conscious of her figure and avoided potatoes in any form she secretly enjoyed their canteen's spicy *aaloor chop* and never said no to them.

Once both of them had settled down with their hot drinks and equally hot snacks Aparajita said, 'So you caught my lie eh?'

'Of course yes!!! I know you quite well…your face tells me every time you do it. Your eyes become expressionless as you look directly into the other person's eyes, just shutting out any sort of inner emotions you might be having at that point in time. As if completely believing in what you are saying. With that kind of an "angel face" look it becomes very difficult to disbelieve you,' Deepanita explained laughing.

'And your eyes are the most important part of your masquerade…guarding your mind and soul, that no one can penetrate, unless you give them the permission to. So you come across as a serious, no-nonsense and straightforward person who can never lie. With such an expression who would think you are actually hoodwinking them.' Deepanita finished describing her friend, and laughing simultaneously.

'What a poetic description! I am sure you can write wonderful poetry if you try,' Aparajita replied in a mocking rueful voice.

'Yeah…and I am sure that you could be my inspiration.' Deepanita further teased her friend.

'It looks like the great liar has opened her books for the day…' a voice from behind interrupted their light banter. It was unmistakably Siddharth's deep and thick voice mocking her; Aparajita realised stiffening all at once.

'So whom have we duped today? What is the latest victim's name? Anyone who would like to share it with me? I am all ears....' the mocking voice continued as both turned their heads to look at him distastefully.

'None of your concern,' Aparajita replied looking up to meet his equally mocking eyes scornfully. 'And mind your own business,' she said as an afterthought, her heart beating faster than usual at the thought of what all he might have overheard.

'Of course, Of course...I am minding my business.' The tall, well-built, dark haired, moon-skinned face adorned with sharply etched classic features wearing an expensive sky blue T-shirt with Levi's Jeans and casual flip-flops, replied.

'You are my business, till I take my revenge,' the twenty-something boy asserted.

'How can I forget the day when you insulted me in front of my father and the entire college and called for your own misfortune to befall you? That too, for nothing I did to you. You poked your silly little nose into my business and played "Miss Meddle". So, now...' He paused for effect '...I am paying back the dues.' He ended mimicking her angry voice.

'Why you shameless drunkard...you were teasing my friend. Why did you drink so much if you do not know how to handle it? If I had not called your father, God knows what you and your hooligan friends would have done to our otherwise wonderful College Charity ball.' Aparajita answered hotly, standing up from her chair to face him fully. Deepanita sitting beside her kept nudging her to let go of the matter. But Aparajita gave her a look to stop appeasing her. Deepanita gave up and slowly kept sipping her coffee.

'...Even the principal was not happy when he came to know of the incident. Just thank your stars that you did not get rusticated from college. If you are a senior then behave like one and not like a five-year-old spoilt brat,' Aparajita continued heatedly.

'Ha...Ha...Ha...' the handsome giant laughed on her face. 'Maybe I am a five-year-old spoilt brat. But you, what are you? I know you quite well...An expert liar! That's what you are. I wonder what all you have lied about to your daddy, dear?' he paused dramatically waiting for her response.

'Well, never mind, I will find out...that is my business for sure. And I sure am going to do a good job of it,' he informed her in a warning tone.

'I have heard from very reliable sources that your dear dad thinks you are his perfect little daughter who can do no wrong...least of all lie for small things. After all you have no reason to. Or do you?' He mocked. On getting no response from two pairs of perplexed eyes glaring at him for answers, he went on enjoying himself completely. '...And he believes his perfect daughter will make him really proud one day. But I will show him one of these days what you really are.' He threateningly paused.

'...Good that your loyal friend Aniket boasted about you and in turn gave out some important facts I needed to know. What did he call you...mmm yeah..."a Pro in lying."' He said feigning to recall and then waited for the effect his revelation had on Aparajita.

'I am sure your dad would be interested in knowing a little bit more about this aspect of your personality. Of course, poor

Aniket realised too late that I am not one of your humble admirers in front of whom he was showing off but just the opposite,' he said enjoying her discomfort.

'Beware of me "little liar", I will expose you and then insult you just the way you did,' Siddharth gave a final warning while he paid for his coke at the counter and then left, leaving the girls standing and looking at his back uneasily.

'Don't pay any heed to him. He is all cloud and no rain. Come sit down.' Deepanita tried to cheer her troubled friend, after she collected herself. She knew Aniket had given away a lot of information about Aparajita in his inebriated state…but she did not know the extent of the damage that had been done. Siddharth's revelation made her quite worried for both of them.

Aparajita sat down finally looking at her fingers broodingly. Her thoughts pondered on how she disliked being called a liar. In fact she hated lying. She hated the fact that she had to lie for the smallest of things. But lying had become so much a part of her that even when she did not wish to, it came tumbling out of her mouth on its own. She could see no other alternative to lying without having to hear 'no you can't do this or this is not what we want you to be' kind of sentences from her focused parents.

5

'You know, I hate lying. I started lying because of my passion for dancing and to keep it a secret from my parents, especially dad. Of course, I got so used to it that I started taking its refuge to solve my other problems in life. Though, I had promised myself to keep it limited to my dance only. But look at what I have become now...' she vented, nearing tears.

Gulping back her tears of frustration she continued nostalgically, 'I still remember how I had felt the day I had discovered my passion for dance. And it was only by chance that I had found out about my inherent talent.'

'Remember...it was during one of our annual functions when you had urged me to participate in the group dance for which I was so unwilling at first,' she said reminiscing the past.

Deepanita not wanting to disturb her friend further nodded silently as Aparajita continued. 'But once I started practising in the dance rehearsals, my interest grew and by the end, I had fallen in love with it. And our performance was so good that it was well appreciated by everyone including our chief guest,' Aparajita said with a sense of pride reflecting in her voice.

'Yes, I remember that day very well. In fact your part won a special mention by our principal for the beautiful way you performed it. And that was the day you told me that you wanted to learn dancing seriously. I remember it all clearly.' Deepanita replied taking a sip of her coffee getting equally lost in the past.

'But my parents were not so enthused when I had told them about it. I was disappointed to see their reactions,' Aparajita said after a while, biting into her hot *aaloo chop* unmindfully and consequently burning her tongue in the process. Lost in her thoughts of the past she did not pay heed to the unpleasant sharp pain in the tongue and went on reminiscing the evening when she had gone and told her parents about her much appreciated performance.

To her surprise Aparajita had discovered that her parents did not share her enthusiasm for dancing at all. Her mother who herself had been a good dancer during her younger days had again just smiled nervously and as always had kept silent after that.

But it was her father's reaction which had made Aparajita feel as if she had done something really wrong. He had looked at his wife, and then at her, barely grunting a, 'Hmmmmm...Okay...Okay,' and had continued with his work.

Aparajita had felt very discouraged at that time but had been equally confused at her father's reaction. He, who would usually encourage his daughter with anything related to her studies or even sports. Still, Aparajita quite keen to learn dancing had kept on pestering her mother to put her in a dance class.

Her mother eventually gave in, albeit reluctantly, to keep her daughter occupied with something during the evenings as she herself was quite busy with her own social activities. But she told her daughter to keep it a secret and never let her father know about it.

'Aupora, he will not understand all this. Even I was not encouraged to pursue dancing once I got married. He thinks differently. For him it is more important to do something intellectual...or you know...study related. He is still okay with sports as he himself did well in them during his younger days. But music, dance and the like he considers as things for leisure and not as a serious vocation. I have not been able to change his mind till date. You are his only daughter and he has lots of hope pinned on you. So this dance school thing...just keep it to yourself and enjoy it while you can...okay??'

She had probed and informed her daughter at the same time. Her painful defeated expression had reflected her inner tussle between a concerned mother and a dutiful wife…with the wife cautioning the mother to not go overboard with her emotions.

'Okay Ma,' the unaware, ever optimistic, daughter had replied, happy at getting what she had wanted for the moment.

However, things about her future became clear to Aparajita once her Sr Secondary Board results were out. 'This was not what I had expected from you,' her father had said looking very upset with her results.

She had passed with first division marks and was amongst the top five students of her class, she tried telling him. 'But Aupora…this is not enough. In any field only the topper is remembered even the person coming second is forgotten,' he had said unsmilingly.

He also categorically told her about his plans for her and what he expected out of her. And of course, dance was not even the last item in his scheme of things. He had been in one of his 'I will hear nothing else' kind of moods and Aparajita hadn't dared to argue with him.

But she had been heartbroken and did not know what to think of all that he had told her. That night she cried a lot and told her mother about her own wishes and dreams. Her mother though understanding had told her gently about her father's expectations from her and had more than hinted her to listen to her father. And it was that day that she had decided she would do anything in her power to continue dancing.

The obedient daughter turned into a silent rebel that night. She was tired of acting like a puppet dancing to the tune of her parents without any say of her own. Tired of trying to explain herself to them for her actions. Tired of faking that she wanted to be a great economist. Her life was under a constant scanner by her parents and their friends. She had to listen to kind advices and 'forced' words of wisdom, on how to lead a successful and fulfilling life. She felt suffocated and jailed despite being physically free.

Even in college everybody seemed to guide her correctly. There was a strong reason for that. Her father made it a point to visit her college once in a while to interact with her professors and check on her progress. All the professors were in awe of Mr Neel Mukherjee, not only because of his name and political status but also because of his personality. He came across as a person who exuded power and strength from every inch of his body when he stood towering over them, with his 6 ft 2 inches along with a well-built physique. His unsmiling eyes would look directly at his particular victim (professor) and his lips would deliberately hold back a hint of a smile which gave the feeling he was enjoying himself thoroughly by making his prey uneasy. So, all the professors complied with his wishes. They did not wish to be seen on his wrong side.

'Come on Aupora, it is okay, don't look so gloomy. Past is past. At least you are not doing anything wrong or hurting anyone. And everybody lies for something or the other,' Deepanita tried to comfort her friend.

'No one is Raja Harishchandra nowadays. Even that brute cheated and lied,' Deepanita said gesturing towards the direction where Siddharth had stood few moments back '. . . to get the information from Aniket.'

'Look into the bright future. Someday you will make them proud with your dance and then they will understand. Then you will have to lie no more…at least about dancing,' she tried embalming Aparajita's troubled conscience. At the same time her own guilty conscience reminded her that even she, was not completely truthful to her parents and even to her best friend from whom she never hid anything at all. But brushing her own thoughts away for the moment, she concentrated on her friend.

'And as far as Siddharth is concerned, he cannot do anything to you. Besides, he hasn't met your father yet. The day he sees him…he will think twice before uttering a word against you,' Deepanita concluded.

'Oh Deep…I hope you are right. I hope my father understands my passion for dancing and still feel proud of me,' Aparajita wished, not quite sure about her future.

She continued, '…Siddharth is just looking for a chance to bring me down. He has been after me the past whole year to settle his score with me but he did not find anything against me till now. But now he has got a point and he will not leave it so easily. Sooner or later he will catch me and then I am done for,' she said worriedly.

Then suddenly, her expression changed from one that of sadness and worry to frustration and anger, as she said forcefully, 'I feel like killing Aniket. Few treacherous glasses down and he is as good as *miyaan meethoo* (talking parrot)…out with all his best friend's secrets. Always telling me he is my closest buddy and can do anything to see me happy and cheerful. But instead of helping me, look what he has done to me??' Aparajita asked her friend looking very upset.

'Thank god, he did not utter anything about me or my dancing. I hope,' she said a little suspiciously. 'Otherwise, Siddharth would have mentioned it.' She continued, gasping for air. 'Besides you, he is the only one who knows that my father does not want me to waste my time learning dance and all. I should not have confided in him. That *ulloo* (owl),' she said forcefully, unable to control her strong negative emotions for one of her closest friends, who it seemed, had lost his privileged position now.

Then worried again about her precious secret she requested her friend, 'Deep don't mention anything about my dance thing to anyone. No one at all!' She said forcefully.

'Don't worry Aupora…besides my mom, no one else knows and you know her. She is not the talking kinds. Besides she knows about your situation. So don't worry at all.' Deepanita comforted her nervous friend.

'…I know Deep…thank you so much. I am worried because of what happened. I mean the reason I do not allow anyone else in my house is only to keep my secret safe. That is the only reason that besides you and that stupid Aniket, I did not let anyone else interact with my parents much. But how would I have known that the fellow will backstab me. . .' Deepanita felt a bit shocked at her friend's wrong choice of words for Aniket, who was her good friend as well. But wisely she kept quiet.

'Anyways, what is done is done,' Aparajita continued, 'Good that he is scared of my dad and does not want to come into the house when he is around. Also we better be careful of this ape,' Auporajita ended.

Deepanita deciding that it was not the right time to defend their childhood friend, smiled gently and nodded in total agreement.

6

'Okay, girls make a semicircle. Deb, Aupora and Deep stand in the centre of the semicircle. Kunal stand between them. Abhishek...hands down please. Indrani, get your body posture right. Bend a little not too much...' the well-built dance teacher Mr Sushanto Mishra, went on engagingly instructing the group of enthusiastic girls and boys.

Sushanto's built was unlike any other choreographer or dancer. With a tall, broad frame, powerful-looking limbs and flowing hair, he looked more like a wrestler than a dance composer or instructor. Yet it was his eyes which looked more terrifying than his body. It was only because of his excellent dance style which could enchant even the devil himself to learn dancing that got him the recognition, popularity and dedicated students. Of course, all his students were as much in awe of him as they were scared of him. But one thing they all loved about him was the way he danced and taught dancing. His passion for dancing was very evident, he taught his students relentlessly till they attained perfection.

THUD!! CRASH!! All the girls stopped dead in their tracks and even Mr Sushanto looked a little taken aback by the sudden noise. 'What was that?? What happened?' Everybody asked simultaneously. There was no response.

'I will go out and check. . .' saying so, the hefty instructor moved towards the main door. His students too, cautiously followed him. It was 6:00 pm in the evening and the students were just about to finish their practice with their final act. The sun had mellowed down. Once outside, they found the huge furniture items lying in disarray. Although nobody was there, it was clear that it was the work of some prankster to distract and disturb the practising dance group.

'Oh it seems some miscreants have struck again. And the guard as always is missing,' said the instructor in exasperation. 'I wonder what these boys get out of disrupting a perfectly peaceful environment.' He said angrily.

'Come on girls and boys…come inside. It's nothing. I will speak to your principal tomorrow. We must catch those disruptive culprits. Enough is enough now.' He said determined and looking rather strangely at the distant college gate, as if expecting someone to be there. Only Deepanita noticed his strange look and tried looking in the same direction, before moving into the classroom again. Deepanita could only catch a glimpse of a well-framed, tall body wearing a dark green T-shirt move away.

'This has occurred twice before, but sir kept quiet about it. He had seen and even caught two of the boys while they were trying to flee the last time. But he let them off after having given them a firm warning….' Indrani, her partner, informed Deepanita.

'…You weren't there that day, he had seemed really angry. Actually it is rumoured that one of them is his younger brother. But no one is sure about it. Both never interact or accept this fact. They also say he is a real ruffian. My brother's friend told us.' Indrani went on chattily.

'Really? What's his name?' Deepanita enquired sounding interested.

'Uh huh…I don't know his name.' But if I am not wrong he is a final year student…from the commerce stream. You know I have seen him sometimes with that Siddharth fellow Aparajita had a tiff with last year,' Indrani supplied further.

'Oh okay! I wonder what vicarious pleasure they get out of all this except wasting our time?' she asked Indrani as much as herself.

'I don't know. Maybe those guys don't like our dancing style or our dance teacher.' Indrani giggled.

'Maybe.' Deepanita smiled back at her friend. She was still preoccupied with the terrifying look in her teacher's eyes but unable to come out with a plausible answer. She ignored the thought soon after and joined the others in the group.

'Okay listen up girls…' their dance teacher said aloud clapping his hands simultaneously to catch the attention of the students dispersing noisily at the end of the day's dance session. 'Around six of the dancers from my dance troupe are leaving and there is a national-level dance competition coming up in December. So I need to pick six others from amongst my best students. So you better gear up…because I will be watching you all. The lucky ones will become members of my dance group and get to participate in this national competition. How's that for a surprise?' he asked smiling proudly.

'Ooooohhh…,' cried the jumpy group simultaneously and clapped enthusiastically.

Deepanita's excited eyes met Aparajita's gloomy ones, searching for her friend's reaction to the wonderful piece of news. This was a great opportunity and they were lucky to get it. But her friend's *'defeated before it has begun'* smile gave her the reply she was seeking. Aparajita could in no way become a part of 'Nritya', Mr Sushanto's dance troupe. If she did, her secret would be out and she would no longer be able to learn and continue dancing. Deepanita nodded in understanding.

7

'Aupora…why are you late from your tuitions again?' her mother enquired as soon as she walked into her house. 'Oh Maaa…please let me settle down first. I am so very tired,' Aupora said collapsing on the drawing room sofa hiding her melancholic feelings.

'Kobita Pishi, can you get me a glass of water? I am so tired I can't even move,' she requested her maid who was coming out of the kitchen.

'Yes Yes I will get it. You do look fatigued and also a bit disturbed,' said the indulgent maid correctly reading Aupora's preoccupied looks.

'Don't bypass me like that Aupora. Are you up to something I do not know about?' Her mother, who had been patiently waiting for her daughter to finish, looked intently at her and asked a little suspiciously.

This might be the right time to accept my lies and tell her everything. At least I will not have to carry the heavy cross of lying to my parents everyday. And then maybe, I would gather enough courage to ask them if I could be permitted to join a dance group I really want to…in case I get selected. The tired and unsure Auporajita thought to herself.

'…Aupora, what am I asking you? Are you hiding something from me?' Her mother's impatient voice interrupted her thoughts.

'Ma…have you been reading too much of that detective book of yours?' Aupora asked, changing her mind. She decided to keep her secret knowing that too much was at stake and impossible to accomplish under the present circumstances.

Then getting no response from her mother, she continued seriously, 'I mean, look at poor me…I am sweaty and drained out with so much of college studies and then those statistical figures my tutor feeds me with. I am almost invisible…that is what you said in the morning…remember? Have some sympathy for your only "almost invisible" daughter.' Aparajita said making a pitiful face.

'Okay okay enough of your drama. Go and change. And make sure you take your bath. It will make you feel fresh. Your father wants us to have dinner together today,' her mother said giving up on her elusive daughter, knowing her daughter's secretive nature.

'Oh! So he is home early today…' Aparajita said feeling a little apprehensive.

Since the time she had joined the dance group in her college she always feared that somehow her father would come to know of her closely-guarded secret. Hitherto she had hidden the fact well from him and everyone else. Deepanita and Aniket were the only ones who knew about it. Their dance teacher had little interaction with the college professors and the principal had a thousand and one things on his mind to even notice a student joining a dance group without the knowledge of her parents. But still she always worried about it and tried her best to keep all the information regarding her college activities to the minimum except about her studies.

Before going to her room she asked her mother mockingly, 'So what is today's topic of discussion or shall I say lecture?'

'Aupora behave yourself! Whatever he says is for your own good. Anyways, I don't know...you will find out soon enough,' her mother replied admonishingly.

'Okay Mom and thank you for your fair warning. I will be ready with my armour.' And without waiting for her mother's response, quickly disappeared.

'Aupora *beti*, *boudi* is calling you,' Kobita informed her referring to Aparajita's mother as *boudi*.

'Dinner has been served and your Baba is waiting for you at the dining table,' she elaborated further, to answer Aparajita's questioning look.

'Oh...I had forgotten about it all. I will be there in a minute.' She got up from her study table where she had been engrossed reading one of Tagore's poems and went into her attached bathroom to wash her hands.

She came down to the dining area soon after, as she knew her father did not like to wait for anyone, even for his darling daughter. '*Hain* Aupora...come come...have a seat,' her father welcomed her in heavily accented Bengali, seemingly in a good mood. 'So how was your day *beta*?' her father enquired in an indulgent voice reserved only for a few individuals close to his heart and Aupora knew she was one of them.

Anticipating this question to be the first one amongst others she was prepared to answer it. 'It was good Baba,' she replied smiling while sitting on her usual chair. 'My Economics professor is happy with my progress. I had a bit of a problem with some statistics but our tuitions sir is very good and made me understand it in a simple form. I practised it there till I got it right. Good thing, I have joined the tuitions with Deepanita. She ended brightly to hide her white lie.

She had in fact joined the tuition classes with Deepanita but was not a regular student. The tuitions teacher being a busy man would hardly keep a check of the number of days they missed. This was a perfect camouflage for continuing her dance classes.

'Hmmm...I don't know...in our times we never attended tuitions and all...but anyways if it is benefiting you then it is okay,' her father said looking at her seriously.

'And what else is happening in your life?' he continued.

'Oh nothing much...just the usual,' Aparajita replied hurriedly not quite meeting her father's eyes.

'Hmm...anyways, I have been unable to visit your college for some time now as elections are just round the corner and my workload has increased. But still in case you need my advice or help for anything do let me know. My daughter is my first priority...after all she is going to be a great economist, making us all proud of her, am I right or not?' he asked her with the same indulgent smile brightening his face.

'Yes Baba, thank you! I am okay now...I will ask you if I need your help,' Aparajita replied still maintaining her smile though her heart shuddered at the oft-reminded thought of becoming an economist let alone a great one.

'Okay...okay...enough of your father – daughter talk, dinner is getting cold...start eating now,' her mother intervened rescuing her from the further queries of her inquisitive father.

After her dinner she kissed her mother a silent 'thank you' which was acknowledged with a peck on her own cheeks, and said 'goodnight' to her already 'engrossed' father, before going back to her room which was the only room in which she felt like herself again.

Aparajita loved her bedroom. It was comparatively smaller than the other four rooms located on the first floor of the bungalow. Aparajita had chosen that room on her sixteenth birthday deliberately. She knew that nobody amongst her family members except Kobita went to that room as it was located in one of the furthest corners of the triple-storey bungalow.

Her parents preferred the ground floor master bedroom and the rest room adjacent to it, due to their easy access to the large living room and the well-stocked library which mostly had someone waiting for the 'Minister Saheb' regarding some party or personal work. He was the finance minister of the state and was counted amongst the most loyal members of the party and quite close to the current chief minister. It was rumoured that if their party wins the upcoming state elections he would be given an equal or more important portfolio again. His important position in the party made it impossible for the minister saheb to move upstairs as he was called upon quite frequently.

This arrangement suited her unaware parents as well as Aparajita. She happily practised the dance steps she had learnt in class everyday, undisturbed for hours in front of her beautifully-carved large swing style wooden-framed mirror without being noticed by her inquisitive parents.

She opened the poetry book which she had left midway and took it to her bed. She opened it to a poem, the title of which touched her heart and she read it again before moving on to read the verse:

Where the mind is without fear

Where the mind is without fear and the head is held high
Where knowledge is free
Where the world has not been broken up into fragments
By narrow domestic walls
Where words come out from the depth of truth
Where tireless striving stretches its arms towards perfection
Where the clear stream of reason has not lost its way
Into the dreary desert sand of dead habit
Where the mind is led forward by thee
Into ever-widening thought and action
Into that heaven of freedom, my Father, let my country
awake.

How relevant for me, she thought to herself after reading and rereading it a couple of times more. Even though it was written by a great poet and patriot at a time when the country was bound in chains…it holds so true for me…and for so many youths like me. I wish I do not have to lie to Ma and Baba or others everyday in order to follow my dreams and fulfil my wishes. I hope they open their minds and see me as I am and let me realise my dreams. With such thoughts and a desire to express her true feelings to her parents, Aparajita fell off to a dreamless sleep.

8

Rrrrriiiiiinnng Rrrrrriiiing. *Oh ho! Why do I put this alarm!?* Aparajita thought to herself impatiently, still groggy with sleep she reached out for it, switched it off with unstable hands and went back to sleep promptly.

'Aupora...Aupora *beti...utho*...it is very late now...wake up!! Boudi is getting very angry. Come on wake up,' she heard Kobita Pishi shouting from a distance like an irritating fly which refused to buzz away.

'Oh ho...Pishi, just ten minutes more...I promise I will wake up in ten minutes,' Aparajita replied and quickly put her pillow over her face and ears to avoid any disturbance.

'Aupora it is already 9:00 am. You will be late for your class. Your father is also downstairs and has been asking about you.' She heard the cursed magic words which had its necessary effect and woke up immediately.

'What? He has not left for office as yet?' she asked making an incredulous face. Her 'without makeup' face, tousled long hair and dark eyes together with her knee-length white night dress with blue flower prints made her look much younger than her nineteen years.

'No...he will leave late today. So you better show up for breakfast and then hurry for your college,' Kobita replied patiently looking at the beautiful face suppressing her smile.

'Okay...okay...tell Ma I will be down in half an hour,' she said resignedly. By now all her sleep had vanished and she was already mentally ready for the day.

DEEPANITA

9

'Deep come back on time today. Baba and Girish are going to Durgapur for some work and Partho will be staying back at the factory. I will worry for you unnecessarily if you are not back on time and then no one would be there in case I need help to go and look for you. That Karthik is also of no use. Only good in the kitchen.' Mrs Srishti Ganguly, Deepanita's soft spoken, roundish mother chattily informed her daughter. Deepanita noticed that her mother looked worried and concerned for her.

'Oh no Ma...I have my Economics tuitions...I cannot skip it today. You know, I have missed a few classes already because of my dance classes,' Deepanita reminded her mother impatiently while hurrying up with her dressing. She liked to mix Indian knee-length vibrant *kurtis* with jeans or slacks. This not only made her feel cool and comfortable but look slimmer as well. But right now it was getting hard to get the right accessories to match her rust-coloured *kurti* and beige slacks. Her curly hair she decided to tie up in a pony tail. It accentuated her neck and shoulders giving her an elegance that was admired by all her friends, especially Aniket. It secretly made her happy to be appreciated by Aniket. Presently, exasperated with not finding the right accessories, she decided not to waste more time and kept wearing the same gold danglers that she had worn the previous day. To that she added her favourite piece of accessory, her artificial gold nose pin. Lastly she applied kohl and a light shade of lipstick. Taking a look in the mirror, she gave herself a confident nod hardly paying much attention to her mother's prattling.

'...Deep, how many times have I told you not to exert yourself so much? You are an intelligent girl and responsible enough to complete your studies before the exams. And anyways, your Babuji and I have never put pressure on any one of you unreasonably,' her mother voiced from the background.

'...It was your decision to join the dance classes and we never stopped you. And now you don't want to leave your dance classes nor your Economics tuitions. Why make your life so difficult when I know you can do quite well, without the tuitions also?' Her mother tired of standing on her arthritic leg for sometime now, sat down on the large single-bed in the room convinced that her precious daughter was over-exerting herself for nothing. Besides, her staying out of the house for long hours worried her immensely.

'Oh Ma...you won't understand. I need to be clear about the various aspects of the subject...and learning in the classroom is just not enough. Besides, dance is what I love to do,' Deepanita replied coming out of her reverie and getting irritated at her simple mother whose world was limited to her family.

Secretly, she accepted that it also gave her the opportunity to meet Aniket outside their college and she enjoyed these small get-togethers even if Aparajita had to be there for all the meetings. She knew, Aniket was besotted by Aparajita and would make the effort to get a chance to meet her again after college everyday. But she did not feel bad about it. She knew (although Aniket had not realised it yet) that Aparajita only considered Aniket a good friend and nothing more. However, it was *her* heart that worked overtime whenever she saw him.

In fact she had known from day one that she was attracted to him. Aparajita had introduced her to him. And though tall, he had seemed so innocently boyish with his slightly curly hair, moon-like skin and bespectacled eyes. She had felt like hugging and comforting him. On the whole he had an attractive personality with many girls wanting to come close to him. However, on his part he maintained a distance with most of his college mates. So she felt privileged to be counted as his close friend. Later, when she got to know him better, she was also impressed by his knowledge and well-balanced views about life. All this made her want him more. And her best friend's reaction towards him had given her sufficient hope to keep her own candle burning for him.

But after the blunder Aniket had made, blurting out things to Siddharth about Aparajita, the meetings became fewer, with Aparajita stubbornly refusing to be part of anything which involved Aniket.

I must do something about this dead-lock situation between the two. Deepanita thought to herself with a sense of helplessness. She knew it was going to be tough.

'Yes…you are right…I don't understand you youngsters at all,' her mother's voice intervened her gloomy thoughts, 'but I know that by god's grace we have a well-established family business and are broad minded enough to let you do as you wish. Girish and Partho are good sons and are supporting your father well. Moreover they dote on you, so you get away with most of the things.' She smiled at her daughter lovingly before continuing.

'Look at Aparajita...she is not that lucky. Poor girl! Being the only daughter she has too many responsibilities on her shoulders. I feel bad for her when she has to hide things from her parents,' her mother opined.

'Anyways...Now my only wish is to find a good husband for you. Seeing you married and settled would make your Baba and me very happy,' her mother went on lovingly.

'But Ma...I am in no hurry to get married. I want to experience life...do so many things...besides Girish and Partho da should marry first,' Deepanita protested mildly not wanting to sound disobedient.

'*Beta* you are a girl and it is better for girls to get married sooner than later. You can do anything you like after that. Who is stopping you?' her mother reasoned patiently.

Ma I also want to work with Baba in his company. I want to learn everything about his work and contribute towards its development. She wanted to say all this and more, but knowing that her mother would almost faint if she worded her real thoughts, she dropped the idea.

'Ma...I am getting late for college. See you in the evening. Do not worry I will come back with Aupora.' And she fled before her mother could say anything else.

10

'Deep any idea about why has our dance class for tomorrow been cancelled?' Aparajita asked Deepanita as soon as they met and exchanged greetings at the college corridor.

'Oh...is that so? We won't have any classes tomorrow?' Deepanita asked her friend in return.

'Haven't you checked the board yet?' Aparajita asked.

'No. Not yet,' Deepanita replied.

Both the girls went through the notice on the college notice board. After going through it once again, Deepanita said, 'I don't know Aupora. Maybe sir isn't well or something.' She looked equally upset as her friend.

'Maybe we can check in the admin office. I guess Mrs Nilima might have the answers,' Deepanita answered helpfully after a while.

'Yeah, you are right...let's go and find out.' Aparajita brightened a little and was about to move when she stopped dead on her track. 'Hey wait...look, there's the cheapskate and he is coming our way,' Aparajita said, her heart skipping a beat as she alerted her friend softly about Siddharth and his friends walking towards them.

Even from a distance Deepanita could make out the malicious smile playing on his otherwise handsome face. She strongly hated Siddharth and his ways. He was rude and was rumoured to have misbehaved with almost every girl in her college. She detested his shameless confidence and did not want to be associated with him in any way. But now he was also her best friend's enemy. And they needed to act fast to get him off their back. But they had been unable to think of anything till now.

'Hi girls...what a beautiful day, isn't it? How are you Aparajita? Anything I can help you with?' he asked them in a mocking tone.

Both the girls ignored him and tried to move away but he blocked their paths and came even closer to block their exit. 'Haven't you learnt to respect your seniors yet? I am asking you something and you both are ignoring me as if I am a wall or something,' Siddharth demanded looking directly at Aparajita, while his other friends stood aside smiling and bucking their friend.

'Well, if you insist…how are you Mr Siddharth Banerjee?' Deepanita asked him instead facing him directly. There was a tense pause. But then he turned towards Deepanita and said mockingly '…And who are you? Her mother, I guess? Hey friends…see the mother and daughter duo coming to college to study together. What a good idea isn't it? *Ek ke saath ek free!* Ha ha ha…' Siddharth laughed out loud and the others joined him in teasing the girls.

Meanwhile seething with anger Aparajita was thinking of her next move. She did not like to see her friend being insulted and made fun of. Deepanita on her part was thinking of ways to avoid any confrontation with Siddharth and his gang.

Deepanita knew that Siddharth's father Mr Kalyan Banerjee was a high-profile business tycoon and Siddharth was his only son. He had been invited to the college on several occasions to give lectures on 'Successful Entrepreneurship'.

She and Aparajita had both attended a couple of his lectures and had found him to be a malleable and an intelligent person though a little overpowering just like his son.

Once, after one such lecture, in a lighter moment during an informal chat with the students he had disclosed that his son was a little awry of him. He accepted that his busy lifestyle and heavy business travelling gave him very little time for interacting with his only son. But whenever he could, he tried communicating with him. However his son did not reciprocate his expectation and always managed to slip away without any healthy heart-to-heart talk between them.

'I am trying to cut down on my travels and workload which are now being efficiently handled by my company managers.' He had elaborated in response to a query by a curious girl (who had wanted to know what he was doing about the deadlock situation). He disclosed all this in order to make his point that parent-child communication is vital for the relationship. And a healthy discussion with parents from time to time is necessary to become a strong individual and a mature member of the society.

After attending his lectures and listening to his conversations with other students, Deepanita had felt a common thread running between Aparajita and Siddharth. She could understand that being the only son of a successful businessman, expectations from him by his parents must be high as was the case with her best friend.

Presently, thinking of something clever, she asked him, 'How is your father Siddharth? I think I should pay him our regards. It has been a while since he has visited our college. And while I am doing it, shall I also inform him about you? And how you like troubling girls in your college or will you move away from our way like a good boy?' She stood glaring at him, knowing his weakness. He did not like anyone bringing up his father's name while dealing with him.

Looking into his eyes Deepanita shuddered as his eyes gave a silent reply to her question. *I will not show my fear to this brute...he wants just that...to intimidate me and Aparajita.*

Since both were standing quite close to each other it was easy for Deepanita to notice the passing emotions he could have otherwise hidden easily from her. The emotion that entered and exited his eyes quickly was one of anger mixed with something like a strong desire for her. She wasn't sure but felt herself go red with embarrassment. Yet, none was willing to give in and they stood like that for a long time locked in a battle of will...unaware of the others standing in a stupefied daze around the two.

Suddenly Deepanita heard a worried Aparajita calling out to her, 'Leave it Deepp...let's go we have a class to attend.' Deep looked at her friend's troubled face and by then confused with her own feelings and the strange reactions of her body towards Siddharth, slumped a little and gave in.

She looked at Aparajita and said, 'Let's go.' She pulled Deepanita towards heself as she sidestepped to make way for both of them. Siddharth who was taken aback by their suddenness, called after her to stop but neither of them paid any attention and almost ran away from the 'completely taken by surprise' group.

11

'What was that Deep? Why did you behave so strangely? I mean you have to be a little careful with those guys. He and his friends have a nasty reputation,' Aparajita scolded her friend while moving towards the class with urgent steps.

'I am sorry Aupora; I guess I scared you too. I promise to take care in the future,' Deepanita replied, a little shaken from her recent encounter with Siddharth. She herself was puzzled at her reaction.

'Anyways let's go to the Admin department after our English Literature class,' Aparajita said putting aside their recent encounter with Siddharth for the moment.

'Yeah okay,' Deepanita replied, her usual warm smile back on her face though she was still puzzled about the recent confrontation.

'Hi…Aniket!!! Where have you been for the past three days?' Deepanita cheerfully asked her bespectacled friend as soon as she spotted him sitting in the first seat for the English Literature class.

'Oh…Hi Deep. I was unwell. Flu,' he explained briefly. And then looking at Aparajita asked, 'How are you Aupora? How's everyone at home?' He said so, not quite meeting her eyes.

Even though it had been more than a week since the day he had disclosed things about her to Siddharth in his drunken state, he could see she had not forgiven him still.

'All okay,' Aparajita replied as briefly as possible and then moved away and sat down in the third row.

Deepanita spoke to Aniket for a while more and then came to where Aparajita was sitting and sat down next to her. 'You should forgive him now. Look at the poor fellow; he is repenting it all so much. I mean, it wasn't as if he voluntarily went to Siddharth and told him everything. That mean-minded boy took it out from him unfairly,' Deepanita ended trying to amend the friendship between her two best friends.

'Yeah yeah…Don't give me that. I know you have a soft spot for him. You can forgive him easily. But not me. He has let me down. Why did he have to tell that evil giant all about me? He knew that Siddharth wants to let me down on the first available opportunity. You know how careful I have to be? If Baba finds out about my dancing or even the fact that I lie to him and Ma, for certain things, he will not only be upset but also suspicious about my extra-curricular activities,' she replied in an excitable manner.

'...He would not trust me with anything. This means no more dance classes. I cannot bear that.' Aparajita justified her stance looking highly upset.

'You know how very important this is for me. And he put it all into jeopardy after a few glasses down his throat. I am not going to forgive him so easily,' Aparajita went on hotly. Then, noticing that their English professor Mrs Nagma Hazaari was trying to locate the direction of the voices, she suddenly became restlessly quiet.

'Okay okay calm down now. We will sort it out later,' Deepanita whispered, giving up on the mediation process for the moment and concentrating on the lecture.

'Come quickly...Let's go and check with Nilima Ma'm, if she knows anything about our dance classes, before the next class starts,' Aparajita urged Deepanita and got up from her seat as soon as Mrs Hazaari left the classroom.

'Yeah okay. Let's go,' Deepanita agreed and followed her out of the class. While going out she turned back and winked at Aniket and gestured him to follow them.

Aniket nodded and after a while came out as well. He saw them walking towards the administrative building and called them from the back, 'Hey wait up for me...I could do with some fresh air too.' And then as soon as he joined the apprehensive

Deepanita and the scowling Aparajita he asked, 'By the way where are you two going in such a hurry?'

'Uhhh...we are going to the admin office. You....' Deepanita started to explain when Aparajita rudely cut in '... and you are not welcome.' Aparajita completed the sentence for her friend. Deepanita looked helplessly from one to the other.

Aniket made another effort. He said, 'Aupora...please *yaar*...forgive me now. I sure am sorry. I admit I had been foolish...but give me another chance. Just one last chance? I promise I will never let you down again. I'll never share any information about you with anyone,' Aniket pleaded looking remorseful.

'Who told you I am going to share anything with you? For that matter we are no longer friends and you better stay away from me. I do not have anything else to say to you,' saying so, she made a move to go.

Deepanita who was standing aside till now butted in on behalf of her other good friend, 'Aupora pleeeeease he is really sorry and he is asking for your forgiveness...please give him a chance. For me...do it this time.' She went on pleading. But Aparajita stood unmoved.

'....Okay, I have an idea. Don't discuss with him anything of importance from now on. But give him one last chance please. We have been such good friends for so long...you can't let it all go just because of that mean-minded fellow who is the main cause of the problem,' Deepanita tried to reason out with her friend.

'Deep, I know how you must be feeling right now and I appreciate your trying to mediate between your two best friends but I am really sorry. I cannot listen to you this time. I told you how he managed to almost jeopardise my life. If that scoundrel finds out about my secret…and really carries out his threat, which seems likely, I am done for,' the angry Aparajita answered her friend in one breath.

Aniket and Deepanita looked defeated and stood their silently unable to say anything else after that.

'Now shall we go to the admin or you want to stay back with your friend?' Aparajita asked grimly.

'Oh yeah I almost forgot…you carry on, I will just follow you…okay?' Deepanita replied. Aparajita shrugged and moved away.

'Sorry Aniket. I tried, but she is really hurt and I think it is best to let it be for now. We can try again after a few days. Anyways, I will see you after college,' she suggested, once Aparajita was out of hearing distance, feeling bad for her friend who looked genuinely sorry for his mistake.

12

By the time Deepanita caught up with Aparajita, she was already talking to Mrs Nilima Chatterjee, a South Indian married to a mild-mannered Bengali Asst. Professor of their college who taught Political Science. She was an extremely busy lady being the administrative officer of the college and wore the 'burdened and irritated' look all the time. Owing to her rude behaviour and sharp retorts students rarely approached her for any sort of query or help.

Presently, Deepanita heard Aparajita asking her politely about why their dance classes had been suddenly postponed indefinitely.

'What???' She heard the lady ask Aparajita pretending to not catch anything her friend was asking.

'Ma'am I want to know why has Sushanto sir suspended our dance classes?' Aparajita asked patiently.

'Well, am I his personal secretary or what? How would I know?' She smirked. '…He informed us through e-mail and he hasn't given any specific reason except mentioning that it was something personal.' She complied on seeing two downcast faces.

'Now does that satisfy you darling? Or do we have some more Question-Answer sessions left?' She asked, in her heavily South Indian accented voice impatiently.

'No…thank you ma'am that is all.' Aparajita replied and was about to gesture Deepanita to move when suddenly she had an idea and turned hesitantly to ask the lady again, 'Oh, could you please pass us his e-mail id or his phone number?'

Mrs Chatterjee looked at her smug face and answered, 'I knew you won't leave me so easily.' But instead of refusing she continued, 'let me look for it now,' saying that she started rummaging through the sheaf of papers lying on her untidy desk.

'Okay here it is…99….' She gave out the number in a hurry. 'Now may I resume my work?' she asked looking at them pointedly.

'Thank you very much ma'am,' Aparajita relieved and happy at her little victory hurriedly noted down the number. Both the girls left after having given their sweetest 'thank yous'.

'Phew! What a relief! But I must say, she is at least polite to you…if you may term "that" as being polite.' Deepanita said equally relieved as her friend and gesturing towards the general direction of their Administrative department.

'Maybe your father's awesome personality and status has had its impact on her as well. If I had gone alone or someone else had asked, she wouldn't have taken so much trouble and would have shooed us right away,' she quipped a little enviously.

'Hmmm, I don't think so, I think poor thing really is overburdened,' Aparajita replied looking a bit preoccupied. 'Let's call him after college,' she said after a while.

'Who? Oh. Sushanto sir. Yeah okay, before our Economics tuition today,' Deepanita replied getting her friend's line of conversation.

Changing track Deepanita went on, 'We have been missing our tuitions for the past couple of days and I am a bit out of touch otherwise also. We need to update ourselves or else we will lag behind the others. But I am sure Aniket can help us with that,' she suggested hopefully.

'You may ask him. I am out of it. But of course you can help me with the course later on,' Aparajita replied, understanding her friend's chain of thought yet outrightly rejecting Aniket's involvement in her life.

Later in the evening they called on their dance teacher's mobile number only to find that it was not responding.

'Let's try him afterwards again…say around 9:00 pm,' Aparajita said disappointed yet hopeful.

13

'Okay…students yesterday we were doing "Measures of averaging and variation," any doubts so far?' a jovial looking Mr Damodar Dhar, who had been an Economics professor himself but had ventured out on his own, taking tutorial classes for the past five years, asked the room packed full of students from various colleges.

None raised their hands or voiced their doubts. 'All right then, I guess, I am a very good teacher…and you all are really smart students who like to study after college hours.' He joked making a comical expression, and drawing a houseful of laughter to that.

'So without much ado let me continue,' he rhymed once the laughter died down.

'Hi Aniket!!!' Deepanita waved at Aniket. He had already walked out and was talking to another boy from their college.

'Hi Deep. I thought you guys will miss the class even today,' Aniket replied with an unsure smile.

Aparajita who had also come out along with Deepanita looked away and pretended to be deaf to whatever was being said as both of her close friends talked to each other for a while.

'Deep I am getting late…Do you want to come or shall I carry on?' she asked Deepanita when she could take it no longer.

'Oh Aparajita please wait for a while. I am taking some notes from Aniket. I can't go alone. I'll have to come with you,' Deepanita replied admonishing her friend subtly.

'He is really good, isn't he?' Deepanita asked Aparajita referring to the Economics teacher later as they waited for a rickshaw to take them home.

'Yes! A life saver! I couldn't have done anything without him. He makes it all so very interesting. I mean had I not been so sure about my future as a choreographer, I would have at least given some thought to becoming an economist and make Baba happy' Aparajita reflected sadly.

An empty auto-rickshaw came and stopped beside them. 'College Street *jaabe?*' (Will you go to College Street?) Deepanita asked the youngish looking auto*wallah*. Aparajita gave him the details when asked about its exact location.

'What about you Deep? You never tell me what you want to be. Actually, come to think of it we mostly discuss me and my problems and very rarely about you,' Aparajita asked her friend after settling down in their rickshaw.

'Oh well you know me...I do not have much to tell,' Deepanita answered her friend with her usual smile.

'You know that in my family there is no binding on me. Babuji has two sons to look after his business and I am their only daughter so they like me to pamper myself well and basically enjoy life. And I guess that is why I am the way I am...I hardly do anything seriously except dance of course...which I really like.'

'I guess I will be happily married once I clear college,' Deepanita said brightly, remembering her dialogue with her mother in the morning, the brightness refusing to reach her eyes.

After a brief silence she went on, 'But to tell you the truth, I really want to work with Girish and Partho da in our company,' Deepanita confessed unable to hold back her feelings.

'But what will you do in a soap factory?' Aparajita asked looking incredulous.

'Well...predict numbers and percentages...just the things you do not want to do,' Deepanita said excitedly. 'It is all so interesting...I can't explain it to you,' she said looking lost.

'In fact Partho da sometimes lets me help him with the accounts books and I am so glad that he gives me the chance. Of course Babuji or Girish da don't know anything about it,' Deepanita disclosed to her friend. However, she did not reveal that her brother himself found the task boring and her offer was a welcome break for him.

'Oh Deep…will you enjoy doing that? You are yourself so creative and what about your dance??? Don't you want to carry that forward? I mean, I think you can become a great dancer too,' Aparajita looked nonplussed with her friend's disclosure.

'Thanks for the vote of confidence; I would surely like to carry on learning dancing but only as a hobby. What I really want to do is help Babuji in running the factory. And accounting is the most interesting and important part of it.' Deepanita gave her friend her usual smile and got down from the auto-rickshaw.

'Anyways, see you tomorrow. And try and call Sushanto sir once more tonight,' she reminded Aparajita as she waved goodbye.

'Okay! Bye…see you.' Aparajita waved back, lost in the recent conversation she had with her friend. *How ironic the situation is…my poison is Deep's dream. And she never told me. Or rather I did not ask her about her plans, dreams and all. This is so wrong. I must speak to her about all this. It has been a long time since we have had a heart-to-heart talk. And this time it better be all about her.*

ANIKET

14

'Aniket, why didn't you take your shoes off before entering the house?' A trim and diminutive figure appeared at the hall entrance and asked him as soon as he stepped into the house wearing the 'object of conversation' on his rather large feet.

'How many times do I have to tell you to keep it outside? I mean after all that I do for you, can't I expect this much also?' Mrs Nishi Choudhary, Aniket's mother asked him again. Aniket did not respond to her nagging voice but instead quietly went out, opened his shoes near the old wooden shoe stand and came in again as if he did not hear his mother but did the needful out of his own free will.

For years, he had been used to this slightly accusing voice and had learnt to tolerate it with a stubborn deafness but never retorted back, as he had learnt it is not what good children did. And he sure was a good boy.

But he also knew that he could never please his parents enough. They wanted more than what he could give, especially his mother. The only saving grace was that his busy father was usually away and whenever he was home he was mostly nice to him. But there was no escaping his mother, who more than made up for his father's absence. Being the only son she wanted him to become perfect in all aspects of life, and her ideal was none other than her own larger-than-life husband. 'You will become just like your father....' she would go on admiringly while putting his slightly curly hair in place with coconut oil.

'But mom that is not fair...' he would mumble softly and try to squirm out of her oily hands. 'Aniket sit straight...let me oil your hair properly,' his mother would insist. Unable to voice his own thoughts freely or argue with his mother about the injustice of it all, he slowly turned into a quiet and reclusive boy especially while in the house, barely talking to his parents and doing things mechanically. They took it as a sign of his obedience to them. They praised him in front of everyone but the cost of those praises burdened him.

The shy and disgruntled Aniket would drown himself in his books to understand anything and everything there was to know about molecules, square roots, phonetics or straight lines. Consequently, he excelled in studies and had his own share of admirers amongst the faculty and his peers alike. But Aniket did not allow himself to open up with everyone. He was his true self in front of only his few close friends who never judged him and took him on his face value. Aparajita and Deepanita were his closest friends. He valued them more than his own parents. His father and Aparajita's father, Mr Neel Mukherjee were colleagues and good friends. And that was how he had met Aparajita. He had liked her from the day he met her. She was ever smiling and bubbly. Very tomboyish yet sensitive. It was in one of the parties at Aparajita's house, that he had met Deepanita, his other best friend.

15

But today he was very upset. Why is Aparajita behaving so stubbornly? He thought to himself turning away his attention from his mother's bickering. I mean, I understand that I did something really wrong...but why is she overreacting so much? What happened to our 'unbreakable' friendship? Why so angry? Why doesn't she understand...that I love her so much...and can't see her getting upset with me? He kept asking himself gloomily with no answers or relief as he went inside his room.

'*Aniket*...come have your dinner.' He heard his mother call out to him from downstairs over the sound of Rabindra Sangeet playing in their stereo system. They now lived in an official bungalow given to his father who was a senior politician. A self-made, prudent man Mr Joydeep Choudhary liked to invest in real estate and had bought several properties in his wife's and son's name, spread all over Kolkata and had wisely put them up on rent. After all, being a government servant, he was entitled to stay in a *sarkaari* house and make good use of his own properties. He also had an artistic bent and liked to listen to old classical music, especially Rabindra Sangeet. His wife too, became addicted to it after their marriage and so anyone visiting their house could never miss the old classical Bengali songs playing on their faithful music system almost throughout the day. And because of his love for all things '*arty*' and his vast knowledge on the same, Mr Choudhary was made the minister of the Information and Cultural Affairs Department. The jovial man also chaired several other committees on culture, music and dance in West Bengal.

'I am not hungry right now Ma...I'll have it a little later. Tell Shontu da to keep my food aside.' Despite knowing his mother must be waiting everyday for him to finish his dinner before she could consider herself free of her domestic responsibilities and retire to her own room for the day, for once, he didn't react like an obedient boy. His voice conveyed his firmness about the finality of the matter. His mother to his relief relented.

Still feeling restless, he bolted the door, took out the small bottle which he kept hidden behind his college books inside his study cupboard. The bottle was half empty already. 'I must buy another one...' Aniket thought to himself as he drank the dark bitter liquid and flinched slightly just before gulping down the entire bottle. This was a sure-shot tonic which always managed to soothe his disturbing senses.

He had got addicted to it since his twelfth standard, when one of his friends considered as an intelligent and popular boy introduced him to the secret of his success. Of course both the friends had gone different ways after their final boards. So his little secret remained in his heart and he did everything to keep it that way. Nobody knew about his addiction, not even Aparajita and Deepanita.

While taking the gulps he was reminded of the day he drank with Siddharth and his friends. His face contorted in anger. *My drinking this blasted whisky with Siddharth and his gang has been a huge mistake. I not only let the cat out of my own bag but also damaged poor Aparajita. She looked so upset and pained today. But of course, what was I to do? Siddharth made me so jealous that I wanted to show off. I am such a fool! Now, I have hit the hammer on my own foot. I really don't know how to appease Aparajita.* He thought feeling morose.

Anyways, whether she forgives me or not I must teach that cheat a lesson for breaking my friendship with Aupora. He more than deserves it. The mild-mannered boy pledged to himself angrily. Finally at peace and resolved in his mind, he went down to have his dinner in silence.

16

Aniket polished off the still hot *machher jhol* (fish curry) and *bhaat* (rice) prepared by his mother with able assistance from Shontu da. He silently praised the sumptuous meal deliberately omitting his mother's association with it. His mother always loved to listen to some words of praise from him. But he was hardly generous towards her – deliberately keeping quiet when she expected him to laud her culinary skills. He had valid reasons. She rarely lauded him for his efforts. His skills were taken for granted. So he made it a point to take her efforts for granted too. His father's case was different. He was not in the scheme of things. He was the opponent. His competitor. And was treated as one. Friendly on the face and as an adversary otherwise.

Mom must have gone off to sleep by now, Aniket thought to himself. After washing his hands in the kitchen itself, he called for the loyal helper of the family who was nowhere in sight. On getting no response from the manservant and feeling restless again, Aniket let himself out of the house, softly closing the main door behind him.

He walked for about a good fifteen minutes till he reached his destination – a semi-lit shop in the corner of an equally shady street frequented by lovers of the sinful liquid. 'Dada, give me a small bottle of Johnny Walker.' Aniket said softly. '*Achha,*' saying so the man behind the counter went to fetch the whisky bottle for his regular customer. *This* chokra *(boy) is good business for me. But if his father finds out that I sell liquor to him he will have me taken care off well and proper.* The middle-aged man thought to himself a bit anxiously. *But I am sure the boy is smart enough to keep his secret.* He eased his mind.

Aniket was about to hurry back home when someone tapped him on his shoulders. Aniket turned to see the person. And though the lights were dim he could make out the contours of a familiar face of a boy, his senior in college whom he knew, Ritesh, 'Hi…Is that you?' Aniket asked hesitantly. The dark face bared its teeth and said confidently, 'Hi Aniket! So, what are *you* doing here?' Ritesh asked him with an evil grin and at the same time looking pointedly at the wrapped bottle in his hands. 'Oh, my father sent me for getting something for him,' Aniket informed his troublesome senior with a faint heart. He was so nervous facing Ritesh and his secret being out that he said the first thing that came to his mind.

The senior, enjoying himself by now just laughed at him and said, '…Oh so your father sent you. Okay! But were you not drinking that day with Siddharth and his gang. I saw you.' Ritesh told Aniket, again making him feel more uncomfortable. 'Yes…once in a while I also drink socially,' Aniket replied red-faced. He had forgotten that Ritesh was also present that day. In fact, he was on good terms with Siddharth and sometimes did hang around with him. Ritesh, himself had his own group which was notoriously known for ragging all the freshers. Aniket had been his victim. He had been so compliant that Ritesh had given him the embarrassing title of being the 'MBRB – most boring ragged boy'. But it was a boon in disguise. Nobody ragged him after that.

Presently, Ritesh having had enough of him, looked at his restless friends who were calling out to him said, 'Yeah...just coming. Just met a junior from college who has come to get drinks for his father.' His voice belied the sincerity in his words. Then he winked at his junior and said, 'Be seeing you buddy...,' before going on his way merrily.

A much troubled Aniket hurried back home silently.

SIDDHARTH

17

'Siddharth *beta*...back from college? How are things with you?' Mr Kalyan Banerjee on hearing his son's footsteps looked up from his work and called out to him. Siddharth, who was in no mood to face his father looked sullenly towards his father and racked his brains for an excuse to slip away. His father got up from the large living-room sofa which had papers strewn all around him and invitingly walked towards him.

Siddharth replied, 'Dad I am slightly busy! Can we talk later?' And on not being able to control his irritation for his father, he added sarcastically, 'and if you want to know so much about my progress then why don't you take out time from your busy schedule and visit my college? It has been a while and I am sure my professors and your ardent student fans might be missing you. So you really should go...not so much for my progress report but for your useless lectures which they find so interesting and even manage to be impressed by them.'

'*Siddharth!!!*' his father boomed angrily at his son's lack of manners. 'What on earth is the matter with you? Ever since your school days...you are like this. Always angry and difficult. Never ever have any time for your mother or me. Yours grades are nothing to be proud of. We have done everything in our power to give you a good life and good education. But you do not even acknowledge the fact. Instead this is the behaviour we get,' he gestured with his hands tiringly.

After a brief silence fraught with tension, he tried again, 'What is the matter son? If something is bothering you why don't you share it with me?' Mr Banerjee tried to get something out from his only son who seemed to have slowly become a stranger to them. Siddharth stood still not wanting to move anywhere close to his father. He had heard this from him several times during his growing-up years. And he had tried, really tried to make his busy dad and equally occupied mom to see things from his perspective. But both had been so immersed with their own work that they failed to understand his longing for them and most of all his loneliness. The one who understood him had left him for good and was not coming back. He mourned for her in private. Her going away made him angrier towards his parents as if it was their fault that she left him.

'Dad let's not start again. I am past that stage now…I have nothing to share with you two except this house and your bank balance,' Siddharth exploded bitterly, moving away hurriedly to hide the carefully controlled wetness of his eyes.

Mr Banerjee, hurt and upset by his son's rude behaviour went back to the sofa and sat down, forgetting all that he was doing, his worried thoughts tried to focus on how to breach the gap between himself and his son whom he loved dearly. *We must do something about this. He is getting out of hand. And he does not even care for anything we have to say to him.* He regretted.

What did I do wrong to make my son repulse me like this. Deep in thought, he did not see his wife of twenty-two years walk in with their evening tea looking a bit tired herself.

18

'Why do you look so gloomy?' Reading the melancholic looks, his wife asked him putting down the tea tray. One look at him had told her that something was bothering her otherwise cheerful husband a lot. She wanted to discuss the issue of diversification of their core business from making steel to building computers. Looking at him now she dropped the idea for the moment. Whatever was bothering him must be very important to make him look so sad and concerned. She thought to herself.

'Kalyan...what is it? Why do you look so sad?' she asked him again.

'Oh...nothing much...just that our son...does not seem like our son anymore. I kept on ignoring his attitude towards us...thinking he will realise with time. But it seems that that has been a mistake. He has moved further away from us,' he replied looking pained and dejected.

'...I mean...he never wants to come and sit with us or share his things with us,' he said. 'Even you have tried so much...haven't you?' Mr Banerjee looked up at his wife questioningly.

Mrs. Ritu Banerjee who was equally hurt and puzzled by her son's behaviour since he had started going to college looked down in order to hide her own frustration and deep concern for her son. 'Yes...I have tried...but I am equally at a loss for his strange behaviour.' She sighed.

'He used to be better than this during his school days. At least he would come to me with his problems and all. Of course those days Ma was also there to help me out with him and most of the things she would take care of,' she said nostalgically referring to the time when her mother-in-law was alive.

'But with her demise, it seems a link has been broken and we both cannot communicate with each other without one of us getting upset or angry. And I never realised he had become so demanding. He would want me to speak to his teachers for smallest of things which I knew he could do himself. Sometimes, quite unreasonable requests. And you know how busy the past few years have been with the company going in for revamping its policies, management issues and opening of new offices in other parts of the country…I could not pay enough attention to him.' She waved her hands in the air to express her frustration. '…And that I think has had a negative effect on him…I guess,' she opined feeling guilty.

Then defending herself she continued, 'But that does not justify his ill-mannered behaviour. In fact I have really tried to connect but his reaction to my well-meant advices are so negative that I have stopped telling him anything at all, thinking that all this is a passing phase and he will come around sooner or later. But now I think it is high time we talk to him before he gets completely out of hand,' she concluded firmly. Her husband agreed.

Siddharth went into his bedroom and banged the door shut. *Why does he have to ask me that question always? It sounds so hollow. They are least bothered about me or my life…all they care about is their business empire. Only Deeda (grandma) cared about me. But she is also gone now.* Siddharth vented, looking angry and sad all at once. *Even mom does things only out of an obligation…because she is my mother…otherwise her first love always has been her work. She never paid much attention to me and whenever it was a choice between her work and me she chose the former. How I used to plead with her to play with me or help me do my project or even take me to the office with her, but she never yielded. She would just look at Deeda with the expression that said, 'Please take him away...I am busy.' And Deeda, not wanting to hurt me would make some excuses and take me out for an ice cream. The grown-ups thought I never noticed and was fooled easily. But I did. And I will never forgive them...nor forget.* He asserted. And then looking at his grim and stubborn self in the bathroom mirror he changed into his night clothes.

Why did I behave like that today? Siddharth asked himself for the umpteenth time, tossing and turning in his bed. He wanted to sleep. But it eluded him. The dinner at the table had been as lonely and dull as he always felt. His parents had again waited in the hope that he would join them but after a while had given up, had finished their dinner by 9 pm and had gone to bed. Siddharth came downstairs once he had ensured that none of them were still lurking around. This had become a regular feature with him for the past couple of years. It hardly mattered as most of the times both the parents were either too busy or travelling. But even when they were home Siddharth refused to eat with them. This was his way of rebelling against their busy schedules.

Now back on his bed...he turned once again...unable to sleep. *What is in that face that pulls me towards her? I have known and dated better looking girls. She is so...simple and...regular...so why??* There were questions and more questions. And the answers were jumbled up and confusing. After an unsuccessful tug of war between his efforts to stop thinking about the girl and his efforts to fall asleep he gave up on both and switched on the TV to distract himself.

RITESH AND SUSHANTO

19

'Ok guyyys...see you all tomorrow,' Ritesh waved goodbye to his buddies. He walked on his unstable feet into the two-bedroom small apartment, (located in a posh locality of Tollygunge), after opening the door with his own set of keys. Drunk and in high spirits he switched on the TV and flicked channels till he got what he wanted. *'Pappu can't dance sala...'* sang the singer joined by an out-of-rhythm Ritesh.

After a while feeling sleepy and tired he got up and switched off the TV. Where is Dada? He should have been home by now. Must be with his ever dedicated dance group or at Mamu's place. He smirked to himself as he went to his room to change into his night clothes. Suddenly the door opened and Sushanto, his elder brother, walked in.

'Hey Dada...you scared me. Did I leave the door open?' Ritesh turned at the noise the door and his brother's walking-in feet had produced and casually questioned his sober brother who looked preoccupied. 'I was at Mamu's house.' He replied quietly without answering Ritesh's question. 'I thought so,' the younger one replied looking very sleepy and uninterested in the conversation by now. 'Okay nightie night...I am off to sleep.' He made a move to go to his bedroom. 'Ritesh...wait. I need to talk to you. This is important.' Sushanto's deep, urgent voice halted the younger and shorter of the two brothers on his tracks.

'Why do you sound so serious Dada?' Noticing for the first time that something was quite wrong with his elder brother, Ritesh turned around to face him.

'The "Lord" is coming.' Sushanto replied quietly.

'What??' Ritesh asked, his small eyes suddenly alert and his well-framed body tense. As if somebody had poured cold water on him to awaken him from his deep slumber.

'You heard it right! Sonju da is coming…he wants numbers and figures of what we have been able to achieve till now…and where did we go wrong.' Sushanto went on, knowing well that his brother was listening intently.

'Mamu is quite nervous. He informed me that we are way below our target. Sonju da is *"concerned"*…and is thus personally visiting our area. Earlier we were involved in small skirmishes with the police…he could handle that and ignored it as being part of our business. But after the Burma *maal* (stuff) got busted…he does not have much faith left in us. It was a huge consignment – more than *12 crores*. And though Sonju da got it freed…it was at a huge cost. Moreover we have been unable to sell our goods…as those snoopy uniformed dogs are quite sure that the consignment is with us and are keeping a close watch,' Sushanto said vehemently.

'Mamu is extremely angry and worried. Today for the first time in so many years he shouted at me. He also said, "…that this time round the Lord won't leave us just like that. He wants answers…for all the mistakes and fallouts we have had in the past…even the small ones." Only a miracle can save us.' Sushanto finished looking extremely nervous and fearful.

'All this luxury...' he waved his hands towards the rich interiors, '...I have worked for, for years...can be snatched away with just a snap of his fingers,' he seemed to tell himself more than his brother as he heavily sat down on the living room sofa.

'When is he coming?' Ritesh asked, by now fully awake and looking as worried as his elder brother. He had heard stories and rumours about the Lord's cruelty from Mamu, about what happened to those who did not perform up to his expectation or who ditched him.

'He is travelling...so he has informed Mamu to be ready on his return. It could be anytime near the end of December...I guess,' Sushanto elaborated.

'Mamu wants us to do something quick. We have a little over four months or so to pull up all our resources and do our best. I am really worried,' Sushanto accepted and looked more scared than worried.

He knew that Lord was ruthless in his dealings. He was at the top of the 'Most Wanted' list in the police files but had never been caught due to the layers of underlings that operated under him and protected his identity. His own Mamu, though a notorious and well-known criminal of his area, occupied the lowest rung of the Lord's drug-trafficking empire. He had spread his empire across the eastern region of the country with thousands of nameless and dangerous faces working under him.

'Dada, don' worry. We'll think of something and pull this off. We always have...haven't we?' Ritesh tried to comfort and cheer up his elder brother as well as himself. But his voice did not sound convincing enough even to his own ears.

'Yes...we have always managed to stay on top. And even this time we must. There is no other option. Go to sleep now. We will talk tomorrow,' Sushanto said with a finality and firmness that reflected in his set eyes.

'Also before you leave...I want to warn you about something...' The dance-class incident in which Ritesh had been involved had angered Sushanto, so he halted his brother once again.

'What is it dada?' Ritesh turned back looking a bit puzzled.

'A couple of days back you and your so-called friends disrupted my dance class again in college. Even after warning you all last time. Why?' Sushanto asked his brother who did not want to meet his brother's angry gaze right now. On getting no response from his younger brother Sushanto went on, 'Ritesh, this is the last time I am telling you – do not do such things. Control yourself. Use it to help me and your own self. Your reputation in college is not so good. You know how difficult it was for me to get you in there. It's a blessing that the principal does not know about your extra-curricular activities and reputation. The day he comes to know...it will become extremely difficult for me to cover it up. Do you understand?' Sushanto asked his brother angrily. Instead of defending himself, Ritesh just nodded silently.

'...all that you are doing is harmful for us. If any of my dance students catch you and most of them have an idea that you are my brother...it will become difficult for me to give explanations on your behalf to them and to the principal. So curb your baser instincts and help me help both of us. Is that understood?' Sushanto demanded strenly. 'Yes dada,' said the subdued younger brother. He knew his elder brother was mostly right, though he could have given an explanation to put his case in better light but this was no time to argue with him.

'Go now,' Sushanto said, turning towards his own bedroom.

20

It was the dead of night. The figure of a fourteen-year-old boy, scared and running away from something was making its way through the darkness. It was dark but the face of the boy was clearly visible. And he was crying. Crying hard. Passing through the dingy and narrow by-lanes of one of the most notorious slums of the area, he finally reached the house he was frantically searching for. Having found the right door the boy started knocking at the door vigorously.

'...open the door, please open the door.' The boy kept calling out till someone opened it for him.

As soon as the door opened, the boy flung himself at the sleepy figure and hugged it tightly. '. . . that dog killed my mother. She...w....as on...ly trying to...pro....te...ct me and my bro...th...er from his be...atin...gs. We...were...v....e...ry...hungry. He w...a...s eating...We as...ked for a bi...te...he started beating us...' stammered the boy crying and talking incoherently.

The not-so-tall figure sat down on its haunches and said, 'Khoka stop crying, stop crying and then tell me...what's the matter?...why do you look so scared?' the figure coaxed him gently.

'I killed that man. Mamu, I killed my step-dad. I hit him on his head with the same bamboo stick he used to kill my mother,' the boy replied with tears of fear and pain but without remorse.

The soft yet piercing rays of the morning sun teased his shut eyes relentlessly till they gave up. Sushanto was compelled to wake up. Deciding he would not get any sleep now, Sushanto woke up quietly, without any visible signs of having had a troubled sleep laced with unpleasant dreams of the past through the night. As if he was quite used to it all. Of course after two decades of seeing the same dream almost every other night had made his reactions or lack of it, as such. Looking at his faithful wall-clock Sushanto realised he needed to get ready. It was time to start the new day and bury the stale painful dream – at least temporarily.

'Hey, why are you still loitering in the house? Aren't you supposed to be in college by now?' Sushanto admonished his younger brother coming out of his room, bathed and freshly dressed in a crisp white shirt and blue jeans.

Ritesh, who still looked drowsy with sleep and was about to drink the glass of water he was holding in his hands stared at his brother for a while before replying, 'Dada what's the matter with you?? Have you forgotten it is Sunday today? No College!'

'Oh . . .' reality struck Sushanto. 'I have got so much on my mind...I completely forgot. Anyways go freshen up; I need to talk to you,' Sushanto instructed his tired and hassled brother.

While Ritesh was freshening up, Sushanto got busy in their small kitchen. He needed to occupy himself with something and besides that he was hungry, he realised. After both the brothers finished having their breakfast of poached eggs, toasted breads and coffee, they moved to their living-room area and sat down on the sofa quietly. Both were silent and lost.

Ritesh was actually racking his brains for different options he could come up with to save the situation. He could not see his brother so harried and upset. Sushanto, on the other hand, had his mind clogged with self doubt and many questions that needed to be answered on an urgent basis.

21

'Dada...I have a brilliant plan' Ritesh broke the silence with his excited voice and a soft whistle. Sushanto, who was engrossed jotting down some figures in his notebook, looked up. He felt a bit irritated at his younger brother for disturbing his important work and glared, 'Please Ritesh, I am in no mood to listen to your crap right now. We are in deep shit and would really appreciate it if you could become a little more responsible and keep quiet while I am trying to work out something.'

'Dada just listen to me once. Then you can decide for yourself,' Ritesh insisted looking a bit hurt at his elder brother's lack of confidence in him.

'Okay out with it. And make it short,' Sushanto gave in, looking at his younger brother's hurt look. *Ritesh might have something useful. After all he is my brother*, Sushanto reasoned silently.

'Well...I was thinking of our contact in North Delhi. . .' Ritesh paused for the effect. 'Go on...how can he help us??' Sushanto asked, puzzled and impatient.

'The pub he runs is frequented by lots of young people. Remember, I had even delivered him a big consignment a couple of years back. Later, over drinks he had disclosed that most of what he took from me was sold to youngsters belonging to rich families. And those kids were ever ready to pay the named price for the "goody". In fact that guy was quite profitable for us. Remember?' Ritesh stressed.

'Hmm. I remember that Punju guy. Chabra, right?'

'Yes! that's him.' Ritesh confirmed nodding his head.

'But, that man is dangerous for us. He had got into a lot of trouble with the police last time. That is why Mamu also stopped dealing with him,' Sushanto informed his brother.

'I know Dada! But he came out of it too. Remember it was all in the papers. And moreover Dada, we do have an extraordinary situation here. And…as far as I can see only a person of his stature can bail us out right now. We just have to be clever enough to do the job well. I mean, have some kind of a camouflage or something…till we deliver him the goods. After that it is his headache. After all, he doesn't want to get caught. Plus, I know he is quite well-connected with the present government. That is why no one has been able to catch him,' Ritesh said animatedly waving his hands in the air.

'Shh…shh…Calm down. Lower your voice. Even walls have ears,' Sushanto warned his brother.

'Think about this Dada. This would be one of the best plans we have had so far,' Ritesh insisted.

'Hmm…I agree…one thing is for sure…we can collect the deficit amount and maybe even make some profit,' Sushanto said after some contemplation.

'But this thing is too dangerous. As far as I know Chabra is still under police surveillance. And you know that the Kolkata police is keeping a tab on Mamu and his activities. They even suspect me. That is also one of the reasons for our poor performance this time.' Sushanto warned.

'But Dada, Lord would not hear any of this,' he said, knowing well when Lord only expected a 'Yes' or a 'No' to his question. And then he drew his own conclusions. Ritesh was sure his brother will also see his point.

'Hmm you are right,' Sushanto replied gravely.

How similar my situation is to Lord Shiva's, who drank the toxic poison that came out of the Sagar Manthan (churning of the milky-ocean by the gods and demons) and lodged it in his throat. Like him, I am not free to act either way. If I gulp down the poison and do nothing about the situation – I will die and if I throw it out, we will get caught. We will be completely wiped out. He thought looking miserably at Neelkanth's (Shiva) picture, nailed on the wall right opposite to where he was sitting.

But there is a ray of hope. A possibility, that if we plan things well, the police might not be able to harm or even touch us. Of course, Mamu has to back me up. And we need the best boys to carry this off. This thought brought a ghost of a smile on his face and he visibly brightened. Looking up he found his brother looking at him curiously.

'Ritesh, for the first time it is smart thinking on your part. Let me check with Mamu if we can work on this plan.' Sushanto got up from his place and came to where his younger brother was and patted him on his back to buck him up.

'Also...think...How can we execute this plan?' saying this Sushanto moved away and got engrossed with the figures again.

Ritesh, by now pepped up by the thought that his elder brother approved of his idea, and at the same time distracted by thoughts of his other friends enjoying a sunny Sunday with beer at their regular haunt, started fidgeting in his seat.

'Dada, can I go out for a while? I need some morning sun and…' he excused himself, leaving his sentence unfinished being well aware that Sushanto might not allow him to go anywhere today.

'And few tons of beer. Right!' Sushanto finished for him looking at him admonishingly.

Getting no response he continued, 'Go but come back soon. We have to go to Mamu's house for lunch today. Okay?'

'Thank you Dada,' replied a happy Ritesh and was about to move when he heard his brother's voice again.

'And stay away from those cigarettes. They are meant for others. Rich, good-for-nothing kids, who can pay, who will pay for them. They can have it as much as they like. But you my dear brother have much better things stored for you in life. We are in this dangerous business for a good reason. And you know that. I do not want you touching that thing. And I warn you if I see you having your own goods, I will send you far…far away from me with just enough allowance to keep you afloat. Is that understood?' Sushanto warned his younger brother with a piercing gaze and a no-nonsense voice.

'Yes of course Dada! I understand. And see you soon.' A timid looking Ritesh wore his worn-out flip-flops hurriedly and almost ran for the door. There were two reasons for his hurrying. He did not want his brother to change his mind about letting him go and he did not want his brother to catch the lie that he was already hooked on to the druggy cigarettes. It was too late for him to quit.

22

'Hey Ritesh, you are late! We have been waiting for over an hour for you,' Montu complained, holding a cigarette in one hand, a Tiger beer in the other. He was not only Ritesh's childhood friend but also one of the most notorious members of his gang. With a skin as dark as coal and the body of a giant he was someone who was revered by his friends and feared by all the students of his college. It was rumoured that the only reason he got into Presidency College was because of Ritesh and his elder brother who were well connected.

The other gang members, some standing and enjoying their fag and few others sitting on the broken chairs of the shanty-like liquor shop smiled and waved at Ritesh. 'What to do man…thank god I am here,' Ritesh scowled at his friend. 'You know Dada stays home on Sundays and it is difficult to get away from him. But today, there was a more worrisome reason to be late. The Lord is coming to meet Mamu and you know why. Dada is really worried and all of us should also be.'

Montu on hearing the name of the drug kingpin looked a little fearful. He knew his reputation well and also knew that the guy would come to meet his underdogs personally only if something was drastically wrong. Otherwise he would mostly call them over to his palatial bungalow located in one of the prime areas of Kolkata.

Ritesh took the 'forbidden' cocaine cigarette from Montu, moved closer to the group and after taking a long puff, looked at them directly and said a little loudly – 'You…all of you…have your last sun, snort and pint today. Tomorrow onwards…it is action time. And I want each one of you to personally look after your areas and increase our sales as much as possible. We are lagging way behind.' Ritesh moved his hands wildly in the air to stress his point.

'We must come up with better figures or else you very well know what might happen. We are not running a charity here. We work, Mamu pays and quite handsomely. All because he trusts and has faith in me and you all. But if we do not perform, he will not spare us, not even me. He will take back whatever he has given and much more.' All the pent-up frustration came out as Ritesh spoke meaning business. The others silently nodded, knowing the gravity of the situation especially as their own asses were on line.

Montu, who was standing some distance away from the group, finished his own cigarette and came towards Ritesh to try and pacify him. 'Calm down Ritesh…we will definitely work something out. We have always sailed through buddy. If that consignment hadn't been caught, we would have made it even this time,' Montu said putting an arm around his old friend comfortingly.

'Yeah…Yeah…I know. Don't lecture me on that,' said an irritated Ritesh. 'But we cannot give that logic to Mamu. Right?? So let's not waste time…we have done quite a bit of that already,' Ritesh said, as he jerked away the comforting arm Montu offered.

Ritesh looked so angry and upset that the group immediately responded 'Let us work out a plan of action,' said one of the members.

'Yes…Yes,' the others agreed. Nobody wanted to see Ritesh upset. They huddled together and gave over-zealous suggestions, asked lots of questions amongst each other and discussed plans. But after a few minutes of discussion they realised that it was not so easy and also that it would take more than a day to come up with a viable plan to get over this serious situation.

Frustrated and tired Ritesh also gave in. 'Let us all go home and think…think real hard. And we will meet on Tuesday evening after college to decide the course of action to be taken,' Ritesh informed them in a no-nonsense voice.

Montu and Ritesh walked towards their vehicles parked in a temporary parking lot. Both covered the rest of the way in total silence. Each lost in the same thought – *How to bail themselves out from this very difficult situation?*

'I do have a plan and I shared it with Sushanto Da today.' Ritesh confided in Montu as they neared the parking lot.

'Oh is that so?' Montu asked surprised, not daring to ask what the plan was.

'But the thing is, there is a lot of risk involved in it. He will discuss it with Mamu and let us know,' Ritesh went on, without divulging the plan to his friend.

'If Mamu thinks the plan is workable and that we can pull it off without having the police sniffing our backs, then maybe we will have to work out its execution. In the meanwhile you keep thinking and let us discuss it,' Ritesh finished as he started his car.

'Sure, sure Ritesh,' Montu replied with a nervous smile and bade his friend goodbye.

I wonder what is the plan that Ritesh came up with? Hope it is a good one. It's impossible for me to come up with a plan that can save our necks in such short notice. This time we are in a real mess.
With such thoughts Montu drove away on his Pulsar.

23

'*Pronam* Mamu,' Sushanto and Ritesh bowed and touched the feet of their maternal uncle (the only relative they knew of) and asked for his blessings.

'*Ki re*…Khoka…Ritesh…How are you both? Good to see you together.' Their Mamu, a five feet four inch stout figure with shocking white hair and piercing eyes smiled and greeted both his nephews in Bengali and then immediately turned sideways to spit the betel leaf in the *peekdaan* (container for spitting chewed betel leaf), that he kept besides him at all times. He was sitting on a well-cushioned sofa wearing nothing but his trademark white vest and blue striped *lungi* over his lean body. There were bodyguards surrounding him – tall, lithe, alert figures cautious of even the slightest of movement or noise made by visitors who came to meet him. And even though he was only Sushanto and Ritesh's uncle, everyone addressed him as Mamu.

'We are fine Mamu,' replied Sushanto for both of them as they seated themselves on the sofa opposite him. Both knew that Mamu was quite fond of them. And being unmarried, treated them like his own sons. But they also knew that he was ruthless and meant only business when it came to work.

Today was one such day. They were called to report on the status and offer a solution for the mess they were all in.

'Khoka do you have a plan in mind?' Mamu looked at Sushanto and came straight to the point. Sushanto, his favourite amongst the nephews, was always addressed fondly as Khoka by Mamu. Ritesh knew that his Mamu loved his elder brother more than him but was not jealous of this fact. He was secure in the knowledge that his elder brother loved him the most in this world.

'Yes Mamu, we actually have a very good plan and I believe we will not only be able to recover our losses but even make some profit if we can really pull it off.'

'Oh is that so?' Mamu enquired, his eye brightening at the thought that he could not only recover losses and save his face in front of the drug lord but could, in fact make profits too.

'Tell me Khoka...tell me...what is the plan? I knew you would have come up with something. After all you are the intelligent one in the family...isn't it?' he said and looked at him with pride.

'Actually it was Ritesh who suggested it,' Sushanto said reluctantly. He did not want his Mamu to feel disappointed at the disclosure. But at the same time he wanted Ritesh to be given his due share of importance in Mamu's eyes.

Mamu raised one of his eyebrows in disbelief, 'Is that so? Our Ritesh has grown up...he can give us ideas...very good very good. I am very happy! So tell me about this plan of yours?'

'Why don't you tell him?' Sushanto nudged his brother to speak who had been sitting quietly all this while.

'Uh huh...No Dada you can tell him,' Ritesh said.

24

'Oh, ho! Don't waste time. Tell me Ritesh, since it is your idea you should tell me,' Mamu demanded.

'Well Mamu, I was thinking that if we could somehow get in touch with the Chabra guy in Delhi. We have done some good business with him in the past....' Then before Mamu could react to that name, Ritesh changed track, 'Actually, most of his clients are youths. And they can pay very well. In fact, he had approached us several times after we broke off with him. But I never told you because I knew you won't entertain him as he is one of the most-wanted peddlers listed in the police files. And he is in their radar.' Ritesh stopped and looked at his Mamu for his reaction.

'Go on. I am listening. Finish what you have to say,' Mamu told him without revealing what he thought of the idea.

'Mamu, he is doing good business. He gets his regular supply from someone else. The last time we spoke he had told me that those guys were much more expensive than us but he had no option but to buy from them. He was even willing to give us a greater stake in the business than last time. He told me that no one could touch him since he was being protected by some very powerful men occupying the top government offices.' Ritesh made his point and not knowing what else to add, he abruptly went quiet again.

25

'And Mamu, we have more than twelve crores of goods rotting with us, which we need to dispose off, besides our regular *maal* which requires to be sold off too. And at this juncture, I think it's only Chabra, who can bail us out at the moment. Nobody will be able to give us such a huge amount in cash...so soon.' His elder brother came to his aid and finished what was left, with a convincing point; he knew their Mamu would not want to refuse in a hurry.

'Hmmm...' Mamu drawled, still refusing to give away his thoughts on the idea immediately. Instead he said, 'Khoka, let's have lunch and then discuss this further.' He moved his hands in the air with a casual gesture and simultaneously got up from his seat. Both his nephews stood up to join him. 'As you say Mamu,' Sushanto said reluctantly.

'Kaku, what have you made for us today?' Mamu asked his old chef cheerfully as they arrived in the kitchen. It was a custom in the house to sit down on small mattresses in the kitchen and the chef along with his assistant would serve hot food directly from the fire to Mamu and his special guests. One thing everyone knew about Mamu – he loved and enjoyed his food. And if anyone wanted to get anything done from him, they had to feed him to a good meal. Also, whenever he had to take any decision on a crucial matter he would always take it after having his meals. Both the brothers knowing this typical habit of his, hoped that the chef make *chingdee maach*, Mamu's favourite dish.

'*Chingdee maach aar bhaat* (prawn curry with rice),' informed the toothless chef to the delight of the host and relief of the guests. 'Good...very good...serve us quickly...I am so hungry...and I am sure both my nephews must be too,' Mamu said looking pleased with the menu.

Ritesh was not that fond of this particular fish considered a delicacy by many Bengalis. So he was very relieved to see the *aaloor posto* and *mushoorer daal*, which were also being served along with the fish in separate bowls.

Lunch was eaten in complete silence. The only exceptions were the sounds being made by the chef while serving them and of Mamu chewing his food rather loudly.

Once lunch was over, they resumed their discussion. 'Ritesh my boy,' Mamu said looking at the younger brother directly as soon as everyone sat down in the exact places they had previously occupied. 'I think your idea has some strength in it. At least one thing is for sure; we can recover our money and on top of it also make some profit,' he said chewing into a fresh betel leaf again.

Then after a pause he continued, 'But before we go further, I must warn you both. A huge amount of risk is involved in this business. Not just Chabra...but even we are in the police radar. One small mistake...and we are all in for good. So Khoka....' He turned to his favourite nephew once again, 'before I can give you both a go-ahead, check this man out thoroughly. Check even the minutest of details and report back to me. Then we will assess whether we can execute this plan or not. For now there is no plan and you better think of other ways to recover our losses.' Mamu gave his verdict with a firmness nobody wanted to oppose or question.

The brothers looked at each other solemnly, then at their Mamu and nodded, knowing there was nothing else they could say or do.

Accha Mamu. I think we should leave now. I will come back to you as soon as we have all the information about Chabra.'

THE TWIN ANNOUNCEMENTS

26

'Okay listen up fellows. A college trip to Shimla is being organised for the IInd and IIIrd year students at end of the month. All those interested, must check the notice board for details,' announced the mild-mannered accounts professor after quickly going through the circular and duly signing it before handing it back to the peon who winked at the class before leaving. The silence of the classroom was broken by the enthused and barely controllable murmurs, at the announcement.

Siddharth sitting quietly on the last bench was the least interested. He loved accounting. But this was a well-kept secret. Even his parents did not know that he was brilliant at it. Despite his love and aptitude for the accounting subject, he had created an impression of an average student by deliberately making mistakes in the assessments and exams. *Such toddlers... can't even control their blabbering till at least after the class.* Irritated at being interrupted in between the interesting lecture, Siddharth smirked.

'Sid, do you think you wanna go for this trip?' whispered an excited classmate sitting next to him unaware of Siddharth's mood. But the stare Siddharth returned was enough to dilute the initial euphoric excitement of the boy.

Another boy too, was lost in his own thoughts, with a similar expression, though for a completely different reason.

Ritesh had also taken commerce, even though he could never make much out of it and was close to hating it. But his elder brother had insisted he opt for it, 'It is important for you to get good marks...if you want a good future. I have been unlucky but at least you can have what I lacked – A clean, happy and bright future.'

But Ritesh wanted to make it big in the underworld. He was happy with the way things were. *I really hope I am able to prove myself to Mamu this time round. If my plan clicks then Mamu will certainly be happy. His faith in me will definitely make him pick me up as one of his close aides like Dada.* Ritesh mused, oblivious to everything and everyone around him. *But how?? How can we execute this plan? I must find out and contact the Chabra guy soon. Time is running out.* Unconsciously he bent his head and looked at his watch and then at the garrulous professor impatiently. As if in answer to his prayers, the distant but distinct noise of the bell announced the end of the period.

Siddharth got up from his place and left the class. *I need some fresh air.* Outside the class he was about to move towards the well-maintained garden, when he noticed the pair of girls he disliked the most walking towards him. They were busy amongst themselves and were obviously going to the arts and entertainment area which least interested him. But wanting to eavesdrop on their conversation he moved closer without allowing himself to be seen. The shorter one was asking the taller one, 'Do you think you want to go for this trip??' Aparajita, his arch enemy, smiled slowly before replying, 'I think mom will allow me if I tell her that the whole class is going! Let's go Deep...it will be fun!' She cajoled her friend. 'Hmm...yeah I think so too....' the motherly one replied. Siddharth found himself staring at her for a while. He wanted his answers so that he could sleep peacefully. She had an air of gentleness, comfort and peace around her. Those qualities made her look rather prettier than her gorgeous-looking friend.

'Help me talk to mom about it. I don't think she would have any problems except that of course you should go.' Suddenly both of them laughed at something the shorter one had said softly. Siddharth could not catch it. The only distinct thing he caught was Aniket's name. Both kept laughing and moved on, completely oblivious to their surroundings. Siddharth stood looking after them for a while, then shook himself, smiled at his own reactions towards them and went out to the garden, whistling.

27

'Listen up. I have good news,' he announced. The murmurs started. All of them looked at him simultaneously. 'As I had told you earlier, a well-known TV channel is organising a national level "Folk Dance Drama" competition, the finals of which are to be held in December,' Sushanto informed the class knowing well in advance the reaction he would get in return. The excited murmurs had already started.

After a brief pause he continued, 'The winning group will get a cheque of ₹50 lakhs from the sponsor of the event and a chance to choreograph and appear in Rahman's song for a big budget movie In fact, he will also be one of the judges for the event. Now, now, wait up. Let me finish first,' he tried to control the spurt of excited voices that were threatening to break the normal volume levels.

'After the auditioning only ten groups have been selected from all over the country to compete in the final three rounds which will be held in the capital. Our group is one of them. So, there is very tough competition ahead,' Sushanto stated.

'But your group is the best sir,' said one. 'We know Nritya can win this competition,' said another. 'Yes sir you will win.' All his loyal students cheered loudly.

'All right all right,' their teacher calmed them down He could hear an exciting thunder of 'wows' with everyone looking happy and trying to talk all at once.

'I am sure we can do a good job to reach the finals,' Sushanto said confidently. He knew there were very few groups who stood a chance against his dance group. The confidence came from the fact that his dance group had the reputation of being one of the best in the state. There were very few dance groups within the country which had the unique style and movements which not only successfully blended the traditional with the modern but were equally enchanting and appealing in form. 'But there is a slight hitch,' he continued smiling; 'I need six new people to join my dance group, as I had told you all earlier. They need to be trained to perfection for this competition. I have a few of you in mind, but I will judge all your performances individually to decide. Does that sound fair to you all?' He asked his excited students.

'Yes sir!!!' they shouted. 'Okay then. You all have a couple of days to prepare yourselves. Also I need two males for voice-overs, as this will be a dance drama. Anyone amongst you or anyone else whom you know who has a good voice and can speak well? Do let me know,' he requested his students.

Aparajita who had neither moved nor spoken till now, smiled at last. It was her 'bright idea' smile. Only those who knew her would have been able to make out that she had something up her sleeve. But Deepanita was not looking. She was as excited as others at the announcement and was discussing it with her immediate neighbour.

That evening while on their way back home together, Aparajita politely enquired about Aniket from Deepanita. Deepanita was much surprised at her friend's changed stance. But rather than probing further she neutrally informed her about his wellbeing. After that both friends covered the rest of the journey in silence.

28

Ritesh dialled the old number apprehensively. The STD booth was located at an obscure place and had two private cubicles. But he wanted to be completely sure that no one was either following him or keeping a watch on him. So he came at a time when the traffic was minimal and the area was clear.

'Hello!' said the gruff voice from the other end.

For a moment Ritesh was not sure about how to introduce himself. After collecting his wits, he asked, 'Am I talking to Kapil Chabra?'

'Who is this?' asked the cautious gruff voice. 'My name is Ritesh. I am an old acquaintance of Mr Chabra.'

'Who?' enquired the sharp voice again.

'Ritesh...Ritesh Mishra from Kolkata!' Ritesh waited for a response and on not getting any, continued '. . . Actually we were planning to host a cocktail dinner in Delhi and I wanted to enquire about the pricing and all.'

'Okay, please call on 099,' replied the slightly mellowed-down voice. The trick had worked. Ritesh had given the code correctly and it had been accepted. Long before, when they were doing business together Chabra had given him the code *'cocktail'*. And thankfully it had either not been changed or had been recognised correctly. Ritesh noted down the number quickly, thanked the voice and let out a sigh of utter relief. *First step – cleared.* He thought as he smiled to himself and paid the booth owner, a legally blind fellow.

Sitting inside the safety of his own car he made the next call to the number given to him by the gruff voice. But this time he used his own mobile and a temporary SIM out of the collection of the many he possessed.

'Yes, hello Ritesh. It has been a long time. . .' said the distinct female-like voice that Ritesh recognised to be Kapil Chabra's.

'How is your brother?' he enquired. Taken aback by the sudden pick up of the phone and the friendliness in his voice Ritesh stammered a 'G…go…good…thank you!!!' Then composing himself he asked more surely, 'How are you Mr Chabra?'

The voice laughed and said, 'As hale and hearty as ever. Anyways tell me what can I do for you? As I recollect you guys did not want to hold any cocktails at my place anymore…so how come…??' he asked a little sharply. Ritesh appeased him by saying, 'It was not in our hands at that time Mr Chabra. Anyways, I have a proposal for you. It is a much bigger party than last time. Is it possible to meet up sometime in this month?' Ritesh lured him crossing his fingers. 'Hmmm…let me see now.' Then after a pause he said, 'I think I will be in Shimla towards the end of this month or beginning of September.' It seemed as if he had put his phone on loudspeaker and was speaking from afar. Ritesh could make out Chabra was consulting his *'planner'*.

'We have a resort there and there is a big group booking at the resort – all filmmakers and all. They need special handling...you understand. So I have to be there personally to oversee things. I will be back in Delhi by the end of the month. Maybe we can fix up something then, okay?' Chabra asked Ritesh finally.

'Oh...that would be quite late. Shimla you said?' The name 'Shimla' flashed through his mind and he connected it with the morning announcement. Smiling to himself he thought...*looks like god is on our side...this could be a natural camouflage for me and I can find out everything I need to know*. Ritesh silently thanked his god and replied to Chabra, 'Actually I will be in Shimla too, early next month, so maybe I can meet you there. Would that be all right?' Ritesh enquired.

'Great! I have no problems. Give me a buzz on 099 when you are there. I am repeating the number. . .' Chabra replied in his sing-song voice again. Ritesh quickly noted it down and sighed in relief for the second time in less than fifteen minutes. Second step crossed. He ticked his 'mind list' as he started his second-hand Swift – a gift from his elder brother.

29

'So are you going for the Shimla trip?' Ritesh asked Montu the next day. 'Do you think we should go? I mean, we have so much of work to finish besides a crisis to solve,' Montu asked Ritesh with an incredulous look.

'Hmm…it can be solved only if we go to Shimla,' Ritesh replied mysteriously.

'Really? How??' asked a completely confused Montu. 'I will tell you. Come home in the evening.'

'Okay!' Montu replied dumbfounded.

Montu arrived at Ritesh's flat at around 1700 hrs, just after Sushanto left for his evening dance classes. Ritesh had shared his plans with him and Sushanto had approved.

'Hi, come on in,' Ritesh welcomed Montu inside the apartment.

'Has Sushanto da left?' Montu asked as he sat down on the living-room sofa, just to be doubly sure. 'Why are you so scared of Dada? And yes he has left,' Ritesh admonished Montu for appearing so fearful of his elder brother. Secretly even he was scared of Sushanto but he never showed it to his friends. 'Oh…no…no…I am not scared or anything just generally enquiring.' Montu lied.

'Okay now listen carefully…what I share with you is to remain with you only…do not disclose it to anyone…remember no one!' Ritesh informed his friend while handing him a diet coke. 'Yeah okay I understand,' Montu replied not understanding anything but promising to keep quiet about whatever Ritesh was about to disclose to him.

'I am going to Shimla to meet Chabra. And you are coming with me.'

'You mean you…' Montu was at a loss for words and his hands which were busy trying to open the can stopped in mid-air as he tried to comprehend what Ritesh had just told him.

'I mean we both are going for the college trip and then meeting Chabra there.'

'Will he be there?' Montu asked still perplexed. Ritesh looked at the puzzled expression of his friend and replied, 'Yes Montu...Chabra is going to Shimla and will be there for some time. Thankfully this college trip is happening around the same time. I spoke to him. He is ready to meet us.'

'Now while I do my job of gathering information about him and his business, do back me up. Try to establish a good rapport with his close asociates to get as much information as you can,' Ritesh instructed Montu.

'This is an important mission. Do not goof up,' Ritesh warned Montu who was nodding excitedly. He was proud to be a part of such an important action plan.

THE GAME PLAN

30

'You know, Aparajita was enquiring about you yesterday,' Deepanita informed Aniket the moment Aparajita stepped out of the class. 'Really?' Aniket looked up hopefully. Deepanita nodded smiling.

'Wow that is great!' Aniket responded feeling elated at this piece of news. *Maybe his best friend had decided to forgive him after all.* 'Let us talk after the class then?'

'Yeah okay,' Deepanita was happy to make her friend feel good. When Aparajita walked in again Aniket gave her a friendly nod. She nodded back before taking her seat next to Deepanita. Aniket brimmed with happiness at her positive gesture towards him.

Later, after the class Deepanita told Aparajita, 'You carry on; I will come in a while. I want to catch up with Aniket.'

'Okay go ahead. Have to look for a rickshaw,' Aparajita complied giving her friend a sweet smile which was usually reserved for special occasions or if she was up to some trick. Deepanita decided it was the former. She was also happy at the thought that soon both her friends will be talking to each other again. She experienced a tinge of jealousy at the thought but brushed the feeling away quickly before moving on to meet Aniket.

'So did she say anything about me?' Aniket asked curiously.

'No, she didn't...not yet. But I can sense it. She wants to talk to you, is just waiting for the right time,' Deepanita said gently.

'Should I go and talk to her then?' he asked anxiously. Deepanita smiled at her friend whose innocence she adored. 'No, no...let her come out with it. You may spoil things if you do it too soon. Trust me...Just wait!' At that their eyes met and before her eyes could betray her feelings for him she quickly looked away.

'Thanks Deep you are a gem!' Aniket patted her gently on the back and moved towards the bike stand.

'Ma I am back. Let me change and then I will come down and have dinner with you,' announced Aniket from the stairs and greeted his mom who had just come out from the kitchen. His mother who was rarely used to his company did not show her surprise but just nodded at him smiling. 'That is good *beta*. Even your father is here today. After a long time we can all have our meal together. I have made *paati shapta* (Bengali sweet pancakes). I know you also love it just like your dad.' She announced unaware that she had just dropped a 'tear bomb' that usually makes people run away even though they don't want to. Aniket gave her a sweet smile of acknowledgement and went up to his room. *He seems to be in a good mood today. That is well and good, his father will be happy to see him.* She thought to herself while going back into the kitchen to warm the food.

Oh so my long lost competitor is back. Now I will get to see him for at least a couple of months in the house. And as usual there will be unending lectures, discussions on culture, art etc. etc. He will boast about his superior knowledge on the subjects to me. Brace yourself buddy and try to stay less at home. That Shimla trip is a blessing in disguise. Now I must go and also make sure that Aparajita goes. I am so happy with what Deepanita told me. She is such a gem. I wonder when will Aparajita patch up with me? I can hardly wait. Aniket thought to himself excitedly while changing into his home clothes. *This calls for a celebration.* He quickly washed his hands, combed his unruly hair and bent down to produce his small bottle from inside his study-table cupboard.

Pouring a liberal peg into the small glass kept on his table; he toasted to his love and long friendship with Aparajita and drank the warm bitter liquid, On the Rocks. 'I love you Aupora. How can I tell you how much I love you?' he said to his reflection in the mirror.

31

If things work out the way I want no one can stop me from my goal. And even the timing is perfect. God, please be with me in this and I will never say – 'I don't believe in YOU'. Aparajita made a silent promise. *But first I must be better than the best to make it through.* Closing the door softly, she started practising her steps. *I need music, this way I just cannot practise,* she told herself when she faltered and forgot the exact sequence several times in a row. *I will have to do this with Deepanita in her house. That way I can even wear my ghungroos and practise the steps.*

'Aupora…Aupora *beti*…the food is served,' Kobita called out from outside her closed door. 'Okay Pishi I am coming'

Aparajita replied and hurriedly changed into her home clothes before going down for dinner with her parents.

Siddharth reflected on the day while driving back. His father had bought him a Hyundai Verna on his eighteenth birthday. Although Siddharth liked bikes more, it was a blessing to have a car for the summers and monsoons.

So they are planning to go for the trip. Hmm...in that case I must go too. I must not miss this chance. Maybe I can find out something more about the little brat. He told himself. And though he tried to ignore it, the desire to know Deepanita more closely had taken a hold over him.

'Hi Mom,' Siddharth waved good naturedly to his mother who was completely engrossed in the newspaper and took a while to respond. And when she did, she was so surprised that instead of responding she kept staring at him for a while. *Her son was wishing her. For the first time in months together, he had actually acknowledged her.* She was thrilled with the knowledge. 'Oh hi *beta*...so how was your day?' Ritu Banerjee asked collecting herself.

'Good Mom. The college is planning a trip to Shimla, I think I will go too,' came the pat reply without thinking. 'Wow, sounds like fun.' Her mother chirped extremely happy about the nature of conversation that mother-and-son were having with each other.

'Come here Siddharth. Would you like to have your meal with us today?' she tried hesitantly.

'Oh no, thank you. You both go ahead. I will have it after a while,' replied a conscious Siddharth. *Why am I talking to her?*

She never bothers to speak to me. I must be going crazy. He scolded himself. And then he left his mother abruptly. Had he turned he would have noticed the hurt in his mother's eyes.

Deepanita changed into her night clothes deeply immersed in thought. *Aniket is so excited at the thought of being able to start talking with Aparajita again. And I hope it happens sooner than later. But what about you?* A small voice from deep within her asked her restlessly.

Me? Well I don't know. Maybe he will find out that Aparajita does not care fore him, but it is I who care for him. I hope he finds it out soon. How do I tell him?? I must give him a sign, otherwise he will never know. Deepanita was brooding on her problem when her brother Partho dashed into the room.

'Hey Deep! How are you doing?'

'Huh…I…I am okay Dada,' Deepanita responded with a nervous smile.

'You look worried? Anything I can help you with?' her elder brother asked looking at her curiously.

'No…no Dada I am fine…just a little fagged out.' Deepanita lied.

'Okay little sis I have the same request to make…can you check the accounts book for me tomorrow? Baba wants it in a week's time, and you know how slow I am with it. Only you can save me,' he mockingly pleaded with her.

'Oh Dada come on, of course I will do it for you. Just give it to me tomorrow. I will come down directly to the factory after my college for a while.' 'Yeah okay, come around lunch time. Girish da is also out at that time. You can collect the accounts book and return it to me the next day? Can you do that?' Partho asked her with urgency in his voice.

'I will try Dada. Just let me see, otherwise I will collect it again the next day and return it the following morning. Is that okay?' Deepanita enquired gently.

'Hmm…yeah fine…just ensure Girish da and Baba don't find out about it,' Partho warned her.

'Don't worry Dada they won't,' Deepanita comforted him. 'Thank you sis. This is quite embarrassing for me to confess but, I love you.' Deepanita laughed at that. He joined in her laughter and then as suddenly as he had come, he vanished from her room.

Dada is such a clown. Deepanita thought to herself smiling. Had Baba allowed him to do theatre he would have turned out to be an excellent actor. Even Girish da had not encouraged him back then…it had broken him down. Poor Partho da! At least he is somewhat back to his older self now. I wonder what will happen when Baba gets to know about my plans to join his company. Thanks to Partho da I already have a hang-of-things. At least I can prove my capabilities in front of Baba and Girish da. But it is going to be a huge task for sure. To top it all, I have to solve the Aniket–Aparajita dead-lock. And also get rid of Siddharth from our lives. She mused gloomily.

32

'Deep can we bunk a few classes today?' Aparajita asked her friend in a rush just before entering the class for their lecture.

'Why? What happened?' Deepanita asked smiling warmly at her.

In Pursuit of Ecstasy • **111**

'Actually, I need to be fully prepared for the auditions.'

'What auditions?' Deepanita asked puzzled.

'The auditions for becoming a part of sir's dance group silly!' Aparajita replied a bit irritated with her friend for being so forgetful.

'Oh okay but Aupora…you want to do it? I mean how will you participate in the competitions if you do get selected, the chances of which are pretty high,' Deepanita asked.

Aparajita just gave her a mysterious smile and said, 'Let's get selected first.'

'Hmmm…yeah right,' Deepanita responded, convinced that her friend had some devious plan up her sleeve to make it to the competitions. Aparajita had told her once that she never gave up or gave in easily. She had believed her then as she believed her now. 'Let us leave after the English Lit class,' Deepanita suggested.

'Okay!' Aparajita answered as she sat down at her usual place in the class. Deepanita followed her.

'Aupora, I have to go to the factory for a while. Will it be okay with you if we go via the factory?' Deepanita asked while boarding the rickshaw from outside the college gate.

'Yeah okay…no problem. Going to meet your dad…is it?'

'No…no…I had to pick up something from Partho da. He might be waiting for me,' Deepanita informed.

'Sure let's go there first. This way I can meet him too. It has been a long time since I last met him. He is so funny…much better than your Girish da who is a ditto copy of Uncle – serious and boring,' Aparajita said making a face.

'Aupora!' Deepanita protested loudly.

'Okay okay...they are nice too...but are not from this generation...you know what I mean?' Aupora asked her friend half laughing. Deepanita smiled at her friend and nodded.

The auto-rickshaw dropped them just in front of the soap factory gate which was closed. Both the girls got down. Deepanita asked the guard posted there to open the side entrance. The guard recognising her saluted and let them in.

'Hey beautifuls!!!! Welcome to our humble abode,' Partho greeted his sister and her friend jovially as soon as he saw them entering the large spacious office. 'How can I be of service to you? Anything you want? Tell me,' he raised his hands in the air in mock courtesy.

'Okay get me the moon and the stars,' Aupora played on.

'The moon and the stars have gone for a wash. They need to shine at night you see...so that you can enjoy the night view,' Partho's repartee came instantly.

'Oh okay, then get me a Mirinda,' Aupora ordered smiling. 'Well that is no problem! *Shombhu... Shombhu...* get two Mirindas for our beautiful guests here,' he called out to the office boy, who was himself a little over nineteen.

'Dada give me the book,' Deepanita said.

'Huh...oh yes...wait I will get it.' He went inside to the cupboard and took out the fat rectangular file. 'Here keep this safely.' She promptly placed it inside the hand-crafted peacock-coloured cloth bag she was carrying with herself.

Aupora was sipping her cold drink and was busy looking at the various pictures inside the office that showed both brothers and their father getting awards by several agencies and companies. 'Wow! Those two look so good together. You look like the ugly duckling of the family,' Aupora joked.

'Yeah I am. I am the odd one out Aupora,' Partho said, his mood suddenly changing from one of cheer to solemn.

'Um…huh…I think I should quickly drink my Mirinda and then we should leave,' Deepanita interrupted, knowing well that her Dada was still sensitive about not getting to do what he really had wanted to.

Suddenly the door jerked opened and Deepanita's father walked in. On seeing him, Aupora quickly started gulping down mouthfuls of her drink. Partho jumped from his seat and Deepanita automatically said, 'Hello papa'. Her father was equally surprised to see both the girls there. 'Oh, how are you Aupora?' Then without waiting for her response he looked at his daughter and asked, 'Deep what are you two doing here?'

'Papa, actually we had some project work. Knowing that Dada is slightly free during lunch hour, we came to consult him about it. Aupora, I think we should go now,' Deep said without waiting to breathe.

'Huh?' said a dumbfounded Aupora looking at her friend and then her dad. Then quickly recovering she said, 'Oh yes…I think we should leave now. Thank you Partho da for all your help. Bye. Bye Uncle. See you.' Deepanita's father just nodded his head in an equally puzzled acknowledgement.

'Oh! What a blessing to be away from him again,' Aparajita gasped once outside the office gate.

'Aupora, he is not that bad,' Deepanita gently chided her friend.

'Is that so? So why did you lie eh?' Aupora asked making a comical face.

'Oh that? You see Partho da does not like to do the account books. I do it for him. I told you once remember?' Deepanita cajoled her friend's memory.

'Hmm yes yes…you did mention it,' Aparajita nodded.

'Neither Baba nor Girish da know about it, that is why I panicked. The hard bound file was protruding out of my bag and I thought Baba might see it and enquire about it. So I had to lie and hurry out,' Deepanita clarified.

'Ha…Ha…ha…so you lie too!' Aupora laughed out loud. 'And I thought I was the only one. But isn't it great that you can chip in for the company too? I mean who would not want that?' Aupora asked her friend incredulously.

'No Aupora you don't understand. My Baba does not want me to work in the company although as I told you earlier I am fascinated by this work and want to work with them. But who can make him understand? You know what happened to Partho da when he wanted to do something of which Baba did not approve. Finally he had to give in and join the factory. Now he is unhappy but Baba is thrilled that both his sons are ably supporting him. For me he has different plans.'

'And what are those plans?' Aparajita asked her, though she knew the answer very well.

'You know, the regular plans Indian parents have when their daughter is old enough to fall into that socially and legally approved age group – The Marriageable age!' Deepanita said gloomily.

33

'Okay class…we will do the selections today. Are you all ready?' Sushanto asked his class.

'Yes sir!' came the resounding reply.

'Deb you go first. Kunal, Deep, Abhijeet, and Aupora you are all next,' Sushanto instructed.

'Sir...errr...we have a request,' Aparajita hesitantly approached the dance teacher.

'Okay shoot!' Sushanto said impatiently. 'Sir, Deep and I have prepared a piece together. Can we perform it?' she tried to meet him in the eye but looked away after making her plea.

'You mean you both want to perform together?' he clarified looking at Deepanita at the same time.

'Y...es sir!' came Aupora's timid reply.

'Okay go for it after Deb.'

'Thank you sir,' she replied relieved.

'Keep your thank yous for later. Okay?' he snubbed her grimly.

'Okay sir.' And she shut up.

'You will know the results tomorrow. Also get me some names for the voice-overs. Okay?'

'Yes sir,' replied the class. Exhausted yet curious to know who all had made it to the prestigious dance group, the students left talking to each other animatedly.

Sushanto stayed back for a while. *Both the girls are quite good. But I must check their backgrounds before I decide to take them. They have immense potential.* With these thoughts in mind, he closed his diary, where he had finalised the names but had to do a background check on them. He walked out and asked the guard to close the room and headed for the administration department which he rarely liked to visit.

'Hello Neelima ji,' Sushanto smiled at the administrative officer who was as always busy answering the office phone. She responded by glaring up at him while continuing to hold the phone and asking him the reason for his visit to the office.

'Hmm...I think I shall wait,' Sushanto replied politely though he was utterly irritated with the rude lady.

'Please finish your call first.' He stood his ground as she continued nodding her head up and down, looking at him urging him to come out with his query.

'Okay. Now tell me Mr Mishra, what can I do for you?' the lady asked him keeping the phone down.

'Oh well, I wanted to just check the applications of a few students who are in my dance class.'

'Any particular reason Mr Mishra?' Neelima Chatterjee asked a little suspiciously.

'No no, nothing serious. It is a routine I follow with regard to the students whose applications come in late and are directly submitted to the office,' he elaborated.

'You see about ten students joined after the classes had already started. As a matter of policy I also keep photocopies of those applications. Last year, all this was being looked after by Mrs D'cruz but I guess after she left, it came onto you.' He further clarified his stance looking sympathetically at the glaring lady.

Mellowed by the dance teacher's concern for her, Neelima replied, 'Hmm...okay I understand.' Then she started grumbling aloud, 'They plan to turn me into a robot...whose sole aim in life is to work...that too without clear directions! Now look I came to know about the file on the dance students through you. I swear, if they give me more responsibilities I will quit!' Neelima steamed out.

'I can understand...must be quite taxing on you, with only one typist to help you with this load of work.' Sushanto smirked and gestured at the disarrayed files lying all across her desk.

'Neelima ji, I am sorry but could you please give me that file?' Sushanto asked gently not wanting to offend the hard-to-please lady. 'Oh yeah yeah sure, let me look for it now,' saying that she got up from her chair and went to the filing cabinet to look for it.

Sushato quickly photocopied the application forms he required on the machine kept in the admin office and handed back the file with a big 'grateful' smile, 'I took a lot of your time. Thank you for being so helpful.' He played the perfect gentleman with her for a while longer. Neelima who rarely returned a smile beamed at him and said, 'Oh you are welcome.' As if waiting for a cue her phone rang and she was her old self again. Sushanto walked out heaving a sigh of relief. *She is better than the D'cruz lady at least.* He thought to himself as he walked away.

'Wow! The girl is quite a catch – daughter of Mr Neel Mukherjee, the finance minister of West Bengal!' Sushanto whistled to himself standing in the long corridor deeply immersed in the papers he held in his hands. *I should have her in my group even if she can't dance for peanuts. The other one has her plus points with a well-known businessman father. I think both will be valuable. Now let me check the others* and he went through the rest of the applications carefully.

'Hmm...' is all he said loudly after scrutinising the applications of all the candidates he had selected. Presidency College had been good to him. Each year he was getting students, most of whom belonged to well-to-do families, many of whom were knowingly or unknowingly part of his dance group which acted as a camouflage for his main line of business – drug peddling.

34

'Fellows, my list is ready. It is with me here. Now do you want to hear the names?' There was a rush of excitement as everyone shouted a deafening 'Y...es sir!'

'Okay the names are – Aparajita, Deepanita, Kakoli, Deb, Himanshu and Abhishek.' Sushanto read out the selected names, loud and clear.

A brief silence followed when everyone – the 'selected' and 'not selected' waited for it all to sink in. Then suddenly the room was vibrant again with excited congratulatory exchanges between the winners and the others.

'Congratulations all six of you. You deserved it. Now you have to work harder to prove that you deserve it!' Sushanto looking at the six of them, shouted above the noise of his students and gave them an approving smile.

Aparajita was besides herself. She had hoped and prayed to be selected in this dance group since the time she had joined it and her wish had been finally fulfilled. She now had the chance not only to be a part of a well-known and popular dance group but to also perform on a prestigious platform.

She looked at Deepanita with tears of joy in her eyes. 'Deep this is a once in a lifetime moment for me. And the best part is, like always you are there with me, I knew we would make it through for sure. I am so happy for both of us,' saying so, Aparajita hugged her friend tightly.

Deepanita laughed and thanked her excited friend equally happy at getting selected. 'But Aupora, how will you proceed from here on? I mean what about your parents?' Deepanita asked, once the initial excitement had subsided a little.

'I… Aparajita stopped mid-sentence, when their teacher started making another announcement and she gestured her friend to shush up.

'I need two voice-overs – male! For the female one I have already decided one from amongst my group. Any boy in the class who wants to volunteer?' Sushanto asked looking at his students encouragingly.

Aparajita raised her hands, 'Sir Sir…'

'Yes Aupora?' Sushanto gave her a questioning look.

'Sir I have someone who is brilliant with voice-overs. I will get him in our next class,' She replied smiling.

'Okay! Bring him, we will do an instant audition for him and for the others as well,' he gestured towards the boys who had raised their hands. 'So it's settled then, next time – auditions for male voice-overs,' Sushanto concluded.

'Deep isn't it great we both are in?' Aparajita asked her friend happily while exiting from the classroom.

'Yeah,' replied a preoccupied Deepanita. She was puzzled by Aparajita's reactions. How in the world would she be able to hide this news from her parents? Sooner or later they will find out especially when she will have to go to Delhi for the competitions.

She was quite puzzled and being unable to control herself, she confronted her. 'But Aupora I am really concerned as to how will you make things work? I mean your parents are bound to find out everything.'

'Hmm…you are right. They will get to know everything,' Aparajita replied still looking thrilled. 'In fact, I will myself inform them.'

'What???' Deepanita's expression showed she was completely at a loss at the thread of events that were unfolding before her.

'Oh you will find out. Don't worry! Let's go home now. And anyway, I have some important work to finish.' She gave Deepanita a mysteriously sweet smile as she walked out into the dazzling sun.

Could you meet me tomorrow during the break in the canteen? Thanks Aparajita. The text message kept staring at him or rather he kept looking at it, stupidly happy with the news it brought with it. *She is ready to meet me now! Wow! Thank you, thank you god!* Okay! He replied to her sms – short and sweet.

'Deep she has asked me to meet her tomorrow.' Unable to control his excitement any further he called up Deepanita to share the good news.

'What? Who??' She was puzzled for the second time in the day.

'Oh Deep, Aupora just texted me! She wants to meet me during the break tomorrow.' Aniket told her half singing, half laughing.

'Oh…' was all that came out from Deepanita's mouth.

She knew there had to be some connection between Aupora's sudden high spirits and Aniket's excitement. But try as she did she could not put her finger down to it.

'Good Aniket! I am happy for all of us,' she replied after Aniket had finished his excited rattling over the phone.

'Deep let's go to the college canteen. I have called Aniket there today.'

'I know,' Deepanita said.

Aupora spoke with her smile never leaving her face. 'Do come. I need you to be there,' she said gesturing vigorously while getting out of the class.

'Okay…okay. Wait up!' Deepanita hurriedly followed her friend who was already out. And a quick cursory glance inside her class confirmed Aniket had already left.

At the canteen both located Aniket sitting at a corner table, expectantly waiting for them to turn up. 'Hi there!' he gestured them to come over, calling out to them, over the usual humdrum of the canteen.

'Hi Aparajita, Deep! So what shall I order?' Aniket asked them once they had settled in their chairs.

'Oh the usual,' Aparajita said, smiling at him for the first time in weeks.

'Okay sure.' He went and ordered three coffees and a plate of aloo chops. Then after placing the things on the table he looked at Aparajita and said, 'Thank you for seeing me Aupora. I am really happy that we can be friends again.'

'Hmm…' Aupora replied taking a sip of her coffee.

Deepanita looked from one to the other expecting something or someone to explode but nothing happened. She quietly bit into her *chop* and found it too salty. *I must stop eating these. They are no longer made the way they used to b*e.

'Deep, Aniket, I have a proposition,' Aparajita started. *Here it comes,* thought Deepanita, still perplexed about what was going on in her friend's mind.

Aparajita smiled her sweet smile. It lit her eyes as both her puzzled friends looked on, at her first and then at each other with questioning eyes.

Then, breaking the suspense she said, 'I am ready to be your friend again. And I will forgive you.' Aniket shouted a huge 'Oh thank you Aupora!!!'

Aparajita gestured with her hands that she had not finished, 'But...but on one condition, will you agree to that?'

'I will surely try,' Aniket answered a bit apprehensively. He had a feeling he would not like what was coming but kept quiet.

'Okay hear me out and then decide. You will help me get permission from my Dad to go to New Delhi for a dance competition for which both of us have been selected,' she gestured at Deepanita and herself and said excitedly.

'Huh! Me?? Speak to your dad??? Are you nuts? I mean, how you can even think of it?' Aniket asked taken completely by surprise at Aparajita's proposal. He immediately regretted his celebrations earlier and at the same time thought he had lost his best friend forever. Even Deepanita was taken by surprise with this condition.

'Aupora you know how scared he is of your dad and you want him to get you permission for your dance competition? It is just unimaginable,' Deepanita tried to plead on behalf of Aniket, who had fallen silent.

She would have continued but Aparajita interrupted her by raising her hands in the air and saying, 'Come on guys, use some sense and pay attention. I did not tell him to go and ask my dad, I said he will help me get the permission.'

'How?' both of them asked in unison even more puzzled now.

'Well simple. He will coax his dad to speak to my father. You know how close they are to each other and moreover his dad loves art and culture and is always trying to promote it in his own constituency. If he puts in a word about sir's dance group and what a prestigious thing it would be to represent Kolkata at a national platform, I am sure he will relent.' Aupora liked the idea even more as she narrated it to her friends.

'But Aupora your father will come to know that you have been learning dance from Mr Sushanto and his dance group. How will you deal with that?' Aniket asked incredulously.

'*Ooofuu* silly you see your father need not know that I would be dancing. I have done voice-overs earlier and it is a dance drama with some background story narration. In his eyes I will be doing that part, along with you!' She pointed at Aniket and continued, 'and though Baba may not approve of that also, with a little bit of coaxing from your father and the knowledge that I will be representing Kolkata at a national level just might do the trick,' Aparajita ended triumphantly.

'Hold on...wait a minute. How do I come into the picture??' asked Aniket looking comical in his perplexed state.

'You will do the voice-over. You are excellent with it and I am pretty sure you will get selected,' Aparajita replied firmly.

'Aupora, you are stretching things a bit too far. You want me to do a voice-over for your dance drama?' Aniket asked looking crestfallen.

'Yes. Why not? You are good. Besides, think of the fun we all will have together?' Aparajita baited him.

'And the cost of not agreeing to your terms is...I lose our friendship? Is it so?' Aparajita looked away from the two pairs of desperate eyes which needed some assurance and wanted to hear a NO but instead heard her saying, 'Yes! You need to pay for the serious mistake you made. This is a good chance to prove that you are my well wisher and a true friend. Do it thinking that way,' she ended.

Aniket looked down, as silence fell all around. And then after a while raised it again and said 'Okay I will do it. But I have a condition too.'

'What is that?' Aparajita asked a bit sharply.

'You will have to come to the Shimla trip and spend the time there together with me. Sit with me, eat with me, read with me, sleep…errrr no…barring that…basically you have to spend all your waking hours with me till the time you go back home,' Aniket informed the two stunned girls.

'Doing what?' asked an astonished Aparajita.

'Just relive old memories,' Aniket stated.

'Okay done. But Deep will be there too,' Aparajita put in another condition. She wanted this conversation to be over and done with.

'Yes of course!' Aniket smiled triumphantly. He had got what he wanted though the deal was a tough one but what the heck it wasn't bad at all. He told himself smiling ear to ear.

While both her friends were gloating over their respective victories, Deepanita was busy with her own thoughts. *They did not even consider asking me what I want.* She was hurt. She knew very well Aniket's feelings for her friend and felt a sudden surge of jealousy and sadness sweep over her. She controlled herself by trying to pretend that things were going to be all right. *Anyways I have my dance to focus on.* Yet her heart refused to hear her. It was heavy and very worried for itself.

35

'Can the boys who would like to audition for the voice-over line up in front of me?' Sushanto's voice boomed into the microphone.

The PA system had been organised, as Sushanto wanted to make sure that he select the best boys for the voice-over. The boys gathered around him. Aniket looked at the other faces self-consciously accompanied with a beating heart.

'Oh my god…why did I get into this? Aupora, what if I cannot get through?' They only need two boys and there are about…eh…nine of us here.' Aniket quickly counted. He could see Aparajita standing besides the dance teacher who looked more like a boxer than a teacher let alone one who taught 'folk fusion'.

'Excuse me sir,' Aparajita sought Sushanto's attention, not knowing that her racing heart had company in her best friend who was silently observing her from a distance.

'Yes Aupora,' the dance teacher looked up from his papers and enquired.

'Sir, errr I told you about a friend who is quite good with voice-overs. He is here today.' She pointed out to where Aniket was standing.

'Okay good…good. If he is as good as you claim him to be, then we will be happy to include him in the group,' Sushanto replied looking at the distant figure of Aniket who felt like melting away form the stern yet curious pair of eyes thrown at him.

The auditions went off smoothly. *Almost all the boys seem to have a good modulated voice. It is a difficult decision,* Sushanto thought. But Sushanto did not want to give away the names instantly. He quickly scanned through the applications filled in by all the applicants. There were two names that caught his attention. One was Aniket Choudhary – son of another well-known politician, the other one was the son of a well-known trader who was into the import and export business. Sushanto could not thank his stars enough. He realized that Aniket was the same boy whom Aparajita had recommended. He looked up at the expectant faces and said, 'Okay the selection has been made.' No one saw the wicked twinkle in his eyes.

Aparajita and Aniket, who were standing together with almost identical expressions of suppressed anxiety, jumped up in complete joy and hugged each other excitedly as Aniket's name was announced.

'Yes...Yes...Yes!!!! We made it!' shouted Aparajita and hugged Aniket tightly. Aniket was pleasantly surprised and extremely happy that the news had brought him so close to his dream girl who till a couple of days back had refused to even look at him. He thanked his stars silently and returned Aparajita's hug. Nachiket who was also selected came forward and congratulated Aniket. Aniket smiled and accepted the congratulations triumphantly – the happiness was for winning Aparajita back.

'So, have you got in touch with the Chabra guy?' Sushanto walked in looking extremely tired and headed towards the fridge and noticed that his younger sibling had not yet registered his presence due to the loud noise of the TV to which he was glued, munching the locally-made potato chips as if it was his dinner. 'Ritesh!' he shouted loudly .

'Yes Dada!!!' Ritesh sat up straight. 'Mmm...You are back,' he said, unceremoniously biting into the crunchy wafers at the same time.

On not getting any response from his elder brother he continued, 'Oh well...I forgot to tell you...I will be going to Shimla.' The announcement drew a sharp response from Sushanto who was standing near the fridge with a water bottle in hand.

'I mean...what is this all about?' He looked at his brother and shouted. 'What are you going to Shimla for? We have a crisis in our hands, and Mamu is depending on us. So what is this "going-to-Shimla" all about?' Sushanto enquired, trying hard to control his irritation and worry.

'Dada calm down!' Ritesh soothed him. 'Have your water first, and then let me explain,' he suggested gently. 'Okay shoot!' Sushanto said, after quenching his thirst hurriedly, a mix of worry and curiosity gnawing at him.

'I spoke to Chabra over the phone. He recognised me and when I told him about our interest in him, he readily welcomed the proposition. He has asked me me to meet him at his resort in Shimla to facilitate some movie crew with all their admin and other requirements,' Ritesh informed his brother.

'Since the timing coincides with our college trip to Shimla ealy next month, I am going there with Montu.' 'Montu? Why him?' Sushanto enquired looking sceptical.

'Dada, Montu and I can check out the ground situation about his gang. Montu is good with such stuff,' Ritesh justified. He knew aggression never worked with Sushanto.

'Hmm...okay! But you should have discussed all this with me before confirming things with Chabra.'

'Errrr...Dada when I spoke to him, things moved fast and sort of fell in place and I didn't want to miss the opportunity.'

'Hmm...okay! But next time discuss all your moves with me first. I do not want any more trouble in our hands, we already have enough to worry about. One small mistake and everything we have earned till today will go for a toss,' Sushanto warned his younger brother.

'I am sorry Dada, I will. Sure,' Ritesh mumbled looking meek but felt insulted and rebellious at the same time for not getting a word of appreciation from his elder brother. *He still thinks I can't handle things on my own. When will he start noticing that I have grown up and am capable of doing things on my own?* Ritesh brooded unhappily.

'When is this college trip you said?' unaware of his brother's feelings Sushanto enquired. 'Early next month,' Ritesh gave the necessary answer automatically. Satisfied with the reply and deep in his own thoughts, Sushanto got up and walked away towards his bedroom.

36

'So Aniket, *kaimon chol chhe*? (How is it going?)' Mr Joydeep Choudhary enquired as soon as Aniket joined him in the drawing room before dinner. Aniket would make this gesture whenever his father would return from a long trip. For two reasons – to please him and to judge his standards – anything new that he might have added to his personality and Aniket needed to be prepared for it. After all to know your opponent well always pays back.

'All okay Dad? College is fine. How was your trip?' Aniket asked throwing the ball to the other side of the court. He knew his father liked to talk about himself and all that he had seen, learnt and taught and done to make a difference during his inspection tours of the governement cultural bodies around the state. If the listeners 'wowed' him for his initiatives, that would please him further.

Aniket particularly needed him to be in good humour today. Mr Joydeep Choudhary prattled on about his recent achievements and how even the opposition party's MLAs had praised him. 'I know Baba…that was really clever of you,' Aniket interjected, coming out of his own thoughts as his father finished bragging.

'So how are your studies going?' Mr Choudhary, realising that he had gone on for a while about himself asked his 'ever attentive' son. 'College is as usual Dad. By the way we are going to Shimla for a short college trip next month! Something I am looking forward to,' Aniket revealed.

'Wow! Good for you young people…study and play…no responsibilities no bindings…' Mr Choudhary replied ruefully.

'How is Aupora *beti* doing?' At that Aniket said a silent thank you to his god. *I was hoping he asks. And he did. I should try this trick more often.* He knew, Mr Choudhary was very fond of her not only because she was the daughter of his good friend but also for her strong liking and interest in the art and culture of the country, just like him.

'She is doing well. But good you asked because that reminded me…errrr…she needed some help from you,' Aniket tried to sound as if he was contemplating whether to trouble his dad or not.

'Does she now?' Mr Choudhary looked at his son self importantly. 'Why? What happened?' There was a hint of curiosity and concern in his voice. 'Dad...you will be very happy to know that Aupora and I have been selected for the college dance team which will represent Presidency College at the prestigious national-level dance competitions. Actually, it is a dance drama for which we have to give voice-overs. We were selected amongst many many other talented students from our college.

'Hmm...very good, very good. I wasn't aware about your interest in dance and theatre. But I am happy,' Mr Choudhary interjected. 'So what seems to be the problem?' he asked attentively 'Dad you know Aupora's dad does not like her participating in such activities...you know related to art and all,' Aniket emphasised. 'Hmmm I know...I know,' Mr Choudhary said grimly and nodded showing how he disapproved this aspect of his close friend.

'So how can I help you all in this?' he asked after a brief pause, in which he had made up his mind to do whatever was needed of him. After all it invoved one of his loves – art. Besides he was genuinely fond of his son's closest friend.

37

'Okay, I have done my part,' Aniket informed Aparajita happily the next day during the fifteen-minute break. 'Now the rest is all upon Baba and it looks like he might just pull through. He kind of likes you a lot. Besides, his pet project to "Get your father to appreciate Arts and culture" gets furthered.'

'That's really cool,' said Aparajita equally happy and excited at the news. She knew Aniket's father was not only the best person for this job but was also extremely persuasive and usually had his way in the end. 'Thanks buddy! I owe you a big treat.' 'No...no...I don't want any treat. I just want you to spend your Shimla time with me,' he said smiling mischievously.

'Whatever!' Aparajita replied, walking away to her seat too engrossed in her own happiness, to notice the gleam of sweet victory in Aniket's eyes. *The day calls for a celebration, I wonder how much of that whisky is still there?* Aniket thought to himself smiling as he sat down for his next lecture.

'Deep I am so happy today,' Aparajita sat down next to her friend busy writing some notes and held her hands excitedly to make her listen to her first. 'Choudhary Uncle will speak to my dad. And I know, he will do his job well. Baba can't resist him. Ooooohhhh isn't that lovely?' Aparajita almost shouted. Deepanita looked at her friend and smiled.

'Very good Aupora, I am really happy to hear that. This is a real big opportunity and we should make full use of it...' Deepanita trailed off, which clearly reflected her suppressed sadness but which went completely unnoticed by her best friend.

'Hi Sid, so how are you?' Ritesh asked his classmate as they bumped into each other in the class doorway. 'Am good buddy. You tell me. You are the one who has not been around lately. Busy?' Siddharth asked with a smirk. He knew everything about Ritesh and his gang of friends. He had first-hand-information that they were involved in the illegal trade of drug-peddling.

In fact a good friend of his who had his own music band had bought some stuff directly from Ritesh. Siddharth knew that Ritesh somehow liked him and so was always cordial and friendly with him. He had even tried to include him in his own gang. But he had politely yet firmly refused. Ritesh had not given up on him.

Ritesh said, 'Oh no, no, nothing much dude. Are you coming for the Shimla trip?' Ritesh blurted out the first thing on his mind. 'Oh that…haven't decided yet. Will see,' Siddharth replied.

'You must come. It will be fun. You skipped it last year too. This is the final year…come on man have some fun. This time will never come back for us,' Ritesh cajoled him having his own secret agenda for Siddharth. Ritesh wanted Siddharth in his gang, he knew the fellow had a lot of potential and was also the son of one of the most influential businessmen of the city. Both facts made him one of the most desirable people on Ritesh's 'must have' lists. And he never stopped trying.

'Hmmm…true…thinking about it,' Siddharth told him, as a warm, smiling, pretty face flashed into his mind. 'Maybe I will come after all,' he said finally. 'Great!!! Today is the last day for registering. Let's go and submit the forms. Here fill this one.' Ritesh became ecstatic on getting what he wanted and to make sure the opportunity did not pass him by, he gave his own form to Siddharth.

'Okay students; please…please…form a queue. This is not a fish market you know. I won't accept any form if you all come onto me like this,' Neelima shouted angrily. The impatient students, who wanted to put in their registration forms for the college trip, behaved themselves and stood in the queue as ordered by their admin officer. The other staff members in the room also looked up and smiled at the reaction caused by Neelima's strong, stern and loud voice.

Ritesh and Siddharth were standing one after the other in the same queue. 'This Mrs Chatterji thinks too much of herself. We should teach her a lesson in queuing up sometime,' Ritesh suggested wickedly. Montu standing behind him laughed out loud and nodded his head vigorously, 'Always hassled and bothered. Never seen a smile on her face. I wonder how Mr Chatterji fell for her.'

'She must be having some hidden talent we haven't discovered yet,' Ritesh looked at Montu and winked. Ritesh went on making fun of their admin officer while Siddharth quietly ignored him. He was thoroughly bored. *I don't know why I am doing this? I mean do I need to do this?* He asked himself quite unsure of his feelings. The face flashed in front of him again. For days he had been thinking about her. Off and on...her smiling picture would appear in front of him. By now he was clear about one thing. He wanted to know some more about her. There had been several girls in his life, but they were all an amusement for him, this time he felt a different pull. And the girl had not even bothered to respond to him. Of course he had never tried enough. He smiled to himself. But something was different about her. She had that calmness and serenity around herself that his grandmother used to have. *So I guess I see my grandmother in her!* He concluded, highly amused at the thought.

'Okay Siddharth...have you filled in the papers properly?' Mrs Neelima asked him looking at his document rather than at him. She liked this boy. But had never showed it openly, lest he and the others, whose company he kept, misunderstood her affection for him. She did not like the others at all. They were extremely rude and rough in their behaviour and had never let a chance go when they could demean her or the other staff members in some way or the other. But Siddharth was different. And she sensed his lonliness and sadness which he masked well under his tough facade.

Siddharth just nodded at her silently, still amused by his feelings for Deepanita. 'Why Siddharth, you smiling today?' Mrs Neelima asked, looking up from the document and giving him a tiny one of her own. Siddharth just mumbled something quickly and moved away as if he had committed a blunder.

As soon as he came out he bumped into none other than the face he was daydreaming about. 'Uh…huh…sorry I did not see…' said the soft voice completely unaware about whom she had collided with and adjusted her specks back in place. Since the admin office was a corner room, it was difficult to make out if someone from the other end was coming too quickly. But Siddharth knew. He knew not only because he had caught a glimpse of her before she banged into him. But also because he had sensed the waft of the soft lavender fragrance she typically used. He remained rooted to the spot for a while, kept looking at the flustered girl wanting to hold her close to him once again. Deepanita on her part went from being apologetic, to being still and then red on the face. She disliked this boy. Yet whenever she met him there was some undercurrent which she did not want to think about. She apologised once again and moved out of his way. 'Oh! So Ms Do gooder is going for the trip too. Good, good we will have lots of fun then.' Siddharth found his voice at last and teased Deepanita to hide his own inner turmoil. She on her part just glared at him and walked away. Siddharth sighed and thought to himself – *Yes going for this trip would be worth it.*

September 2008

THE TRIP TO SHIMLA

38

'Hey Aupora, wait up for me. It sure is wet, windy and chilly here. But lovely isn't it?' the visibly shivering Aniket asked Aparajita. He looked up and took in the pastel evening sky, the brightly lit mountains and the noisy homeward-bound birds.

'Looks like a well-organised, natural light-and-sound show,' he said mesmerised. Aparajita nodded, taken in by the scenic beauty. She was already outside their old yet neat and beautifully-maintained hotel that sat prettily perched on a hilltop, a few kilometres away from the main street and market place of Shimla. Aniket glanced at the lost Aparajita and found her looking extremely beautiful and childlike all at once in her warm leggings and knee-length light woollen peach top. He wanted to hug her, but knew he could not. Before I leave this place I am going to confess my love to her, he pledged to himself. *Can't go on living like this.* Just then Aparajita looked at him and said, 'Hey, stop dreaming let's go,' she said, smiling fondly at him. Both friends hurried to join the others for an evening stroll to the ever popular and absolutely must-visit – 'mall' of the bustling hilly town.

There were around seventy-five students who had registered for this trip. Accompanying them were five equally happy professors to oversee the trip's nitty-gritties. Not that the students cared much. The trip was meant to make students feel free and have loads of fun. Everyone knew this agenda clearly, none waited or wasted their time listening to their temporary guardians, who looked a bit wary but equally happy to leave their wards alone.

Everything had been pre-arranged to near perfection. They had all taken the supremely comfortable and high speed Kolkata Rajdhani to New Delhi. Then, after a brief halt at the New Delhi station they took the Himalayan Queen that had been booked till Kalka – the small town named after Goddess Kali and situated at the foothill of the Himalayas. From Kalka, the narrow gauge train (or the toy train) took the tired, sleepy yet excited and noisy group through the spell-binding picturesque valley across 102 tunnels to their hilly destination. The trip was to be of fifteen days, including a short halt at Delhi on the return leg. Each and every member in the group seemed in high spirits. After all, such holidays did help to break free from the mundane and the routine. But very few knew that many in the group had their own personal agendas – some of the heart and some of the mind.

'Deep, how did you manage to convince her mom?' Aniket enquired as he huffed behind the excited girls who were looking and taking pictures of the several colonial buildings which towered the mall, clearly reflecting its British heritage.

'Oh, it was easy. I told her that besides me, her darling Aniket was also going for the trip. And you know how she adores you. She thinks you are the most sensible person after her who can take care of Aparajita,' Deepanita added sardonically, clicking away with her Nikon – Coolpix happily.

'Of course we know better.' Deep smiled at him and played it light to hide her emotions. *Oh how she herself adored him! Why can't he see that it is I who care for him and not Aparajita?* She thought to herself with a tinge of regret. The completely oblivious Aniket smiled back at her. Distracted for a moment by his boyish smile, she came back to reality again.

'Uh...huh...I also told Aunty that this trip will be quite interesting coz on our way back we will even stop at Delhi for a visit to the Rashtrapati Bhawan, meet the president and and even see the Parliament in action,' Deepanita mumbled. 'Her mom asked her dad, who you know readily agreed. After all, his daughter would get a brief insight into how the Indian political set-up works...and so here we are!' Deepanita finished triumphantly lifting her arms up towards the distant mountains, faking a cheerful smile.

'But that was a lie. We are not going to Rashtrapati Bhawan. But we will see a bit of Delhi on our return,' remarked a worried Aniket still shivering. He was not used to such icy breeze. And now the only thing he found himself disliking about Shimla was the weather. It made him look stupid with his chattering teeth and his body refusing to obey his stern mind to stop shivering in a silly way. All the others seemed okay, except for few girls in the group who looked equally sick and funny.

'Oh ho stupid. They don't know that. We will tell them that there was no time or cook something else up. Right Aupora?' Deepanita replied, looking coolly at Aniket and then joined her best friend who was standing a little away from them and was lost in her own thoughts, enjoying the surroundings.

'...Hmmm yes, forget it all now. Just enjoy this. Isn't it all so beautiful?' Aparajita said looking at the majestic mountains, some of which glistened brightly, surrounded by equally dominant ones which loomed darkly over the bright ones.

Siddharth along with a few other boys was on the other side of the street just opposite the unaware Deepanita and her friends. While she was chatting with them, Siddharth wanted to know what were they all so engrossed about, stopped walking and told the other boys to carry on. Deepanita's profile was visible from where he was standing and since his side of the street did not have enough light he decided to stay in the shadows at a safe distance and eavesdrop on the friends. *After all this might throw some light on two of the biggest mysteries I am trying to solve,* he thought to himself mischievously.

Her face has so many emotions all at once, he thought to himself as he stood silently to overhear the friends. *Does she like Aniket? How warmly she smiles at him, but our dear friend clearly has someone else in mind, poor girl. I hope she knows. How lovely she looks…so peaceful and pure…just like…*he stopped himself short from naming the one person whom he had loved since childhood but who was no more. *What a silly thought!* He admonished himself firmly. *But good I stayed back atleast now I know a bit more about our Ms 'Lie-me-not'. Her parents are not okay with sending her out, unless her best friends also chip in and lie for her. Hmmmm. This might come handy some time.* He filed the information in his memory file.

How can Deepanita be so motherly and protective about this snooty Aupora? Just don't get it! Siddharth mused. He stood there for a little while looking at the girl for whom he felt a strange pull he could not name. But restless and a little worried with his own disturbing thoughts, he moved away, keeping to the shadows. But before he moved away, the smiling Deepanita spotted him as that particular area was well lit. Their eyes met for a brief while and despite himself, Siddharth smiled at her, genuinely, and found himself looking into a pair of steel-rimmed, yet large, clear and innocently beautiful eyes that looked away as soon as they met his. Siddharth felt that strong pull again, confused, he walked away hurriedly.

39

'Montu hurry up, let us go and do a recce of the area. What was the name of that resort again?' Ritesh called out to his childhood friend as soon as he got out of the hotel building with a purposeful stride. 'The Lord's Holiday Manor or something of that sort,' replied the hurrying giant following his friend and leader faithfully.

'*Uuuffffoh.* You come across it after crossing the mall,' he said annoyingly, studying the directions on the piece of paper he held in his hands.

'Don't worry, it is a very busy place this time of the evening, plus the low lights around the area will help us play hide-and-seek well. Now come on, hurry up,' Ritesh informed him.

'Why aren't there any rickshaws here?' Montu grumbled as his large bulk panted behind the lithe and fit frame of his friend.

'Remember keep a very low profile. I won't be coming with you. You will have to go all alone as I told you. So don't goof up. I will walk in separately and do my own bit. OK?' Ritesh checked a bit uncertain about Montu.

'And don't let anyone know we are here with the college group. Check each and every corner of the area. Interact with the bell boys, cooks, housekeeping guys, anyone who can give you some information about Chabra. But DON'T...I repeat DON'T raise brows! Do it very casually, yet cautiously. Understood?' Ritesh warned his confidant.

The equally grim partner nodded in understanding. He knew this was one of the most important assignments he had been given. If he performed well, he would not only please Ritesh but also get noticed by Sushanto and Mamu for other important and well-paying assignments which he desperately wanted. After all, it was his dream to own a SUV of his own. But for that he first needed to have a big pocket, a real big one. And secondly to fill it up well, this was the only way to do it.

'Hello, good evening sir. How may I help you?' asked a young girl at the reception counter. 'Oh I spoke to one Mr Guleria. I am here to check a few places for a marriage party. Actually my sister is getting married to one of the boys from your town,' Montu looked at the girl and gave her a shy smile who smiled back encouragingly. Initially the girl had felt a bit uncomfortable at seeing a huge dark Indian version of the Hulk standing in front of her. She relaxed visibly once the Hulk started talking to her in a friendly tone. '...And the boy's side wanted the marriage to be organised here. I am pretty new to the area. They tell me your resort is quite popular for marriage parties.' Unaware about the girl's thoughts, Montu carried on, playing his part to perfection. 'Oh yes sir...it is indeed. You will soon see.' The girl answered sweetly as she picked up the phone to call her senior colleague Ajay Guleria who handled banquet enquiries.

Ritesh on his part moved in quietly and went past the reception unnoticed. A little further down the hall he enquired about the directions for the hotel restaurant. The teenaged bellboy, who looked happy to help, guided him to the place courteously. 'Hello, good evening sir!' welcomed a cultured voice which Ritesh assumed to belong to the restaurant manager or some senior employee of the hotel. The well-dressed man was standing just inside the restaurant door.

'Oh...hello...A nice place you have here,' Ritesh said returning the received smile.

'Thank you sir. And you are looking for a table for??' asked the man raising his bushy brows in a polite questioning gesture.

'Oh just for me as of now. But I have a gang of friends strolling in the mall, who would surely want to come and have dinner here,' Ritesh answered. 'You see, an old friend who stayed with you earlier recommended your restaurant. I thought, I would just check it out myself first and then recommend it to others,' Ritesh said as his quick and sharp eyes took in the interiors and also at the same time noticed that he was indeed talking to the restaurant manager whose golden name plate addressed him as Ravi Kumar. Not wanting to interrupt the amiable and chatty middle-aged Ravi, Ritesh went on with his cock-and-bull story. '...He had asked me to try out some of your fresh-water fish dishes'. Ritesh kept his wide smile on.

'Oh yes!!! He was right in recommending us, sir. We have a river just next to our hotel and most of our fish come from there. Also our old chef is well known for his different yet excellent style of fish preparations,' cajoled the delighted manager.

'Hmm. Good...good! The way you describe it makes me feel famished,' Ritesh cheered on in a fake voice.

'So tell me, who owns this place?' Ritesh enquired further, as he was shown a table by the window overlooking the river in the dark but which reflected the silver moon beautifully from this place.

'Sir, the resort belongs to Mr K. Chabra, a businessman from Delhi. He took it over about three years back from the original owners of this place who could not manage the property themselves.' He replied, happy to help his guest who looked so interested in the property. 'And I have served under both the owners,' he added proudly.

'Wow! That is so good. You must be really great with your work.' Ritesh flattered the man further, 'It is an honour to meet you sir.' Ritesh looked into Ravi's eyes, smiled and shook hands with him. The 'Sir' and the 'handshake' bit did the trick.

Ravi looked back at his guest self importantly and replied, 'Yes, I have given my best to the resort. I am one of their oldest employees and have seen many ups and downs but never gave up,' he informed in one breath. 'In fact the old Mr Sharma loved me like his own son and gave me a free rein in other areas too, that is also one of the reasons why all the hotel staff including our new owner respects me and my ideas so much. He has made changes and done renovations everywhere except in the general layout, which was my suggestion again and this restaurant, which is completely my baby,' he said emotionally.

'When you walk in here you can feel yourself cocooned into the old world, away from the hustle-bustle and noisy Shimla. Mind you the city was not always like this, but you know how in the name of development nature has to suffer,' he made a sour face at that. Ritesh though bored a bit showed his acute concern and nodded in total agreement.

'Anyways, up here you will find yourself up-close-and-personal with nature. Even from inside the restaurant the scenic beauty is so very captivating. It can charm even the dullest of persons. I have worked hard to ensure that none of this is disturbed or destroyed with the so-called modern interiors and designs. Thankfully they listened to me. And the business is thriving. We have many *firangis* who come down to our resort, just to feel the lovely ambience and taste our sumptuous food,' the self engrossed Ravi went on and on.

'Errrrr...so very interesting, I tell you, why don't you join me for a small drink?' Ritesh intervened and lured him further.

'Oh thank you...thanks for your offer sir. But you see I cannot drink while on duty.' Ravi looked pleased and embarrassed at the same time. 'I understand and respect that completely sir. You are the boss. You make the rules. But I have really developed an admiration for this beautifully maintained resort and for people, like you, who are so nature friendly and run this place so efficiently. I really would like to know a little more.'

'And to tell you honestly, I am a travel writer and would love to describe and write an exclusive article on this place. Maybe later, if you allow me I could click a few pictures also.' And before the man could think or say anything else he went on, 'I find your ideas quite interesting.' Ritesh fuelled the manager's ego further.

The simple man was delighted but a bit wary. But after a few more rounds of 'ego pumping' Ritesh convinced Ravi that a drink or two was not at all out of place, in fact he deserved it.

Ravi called out to his junior who was ushering in other guests at the entrance. As the boy came up to him, he gave his orders authoritatively once the boy had wished his senior and the guest the customary 'good evening sir' in a cheerful voice. He informed the boy that he would be taking a short break to spend some time with Ritesh who was his personal guest. 'So you take charge and if and only if there is some trouble-shooting required you call me. Okay?' he ordered the young fellow in a no-nonsense voice. 'Right sir! Please go ahead. I will see to it,' replied the obedient fellow.

Things are going perfectly, Ritesh congratulated himself. He gave Ravi a smile of gratitude, hiding his ulterior motives well. 'Can I get a pen and paper too? I want to jot down all the points,' Ritesh requested the boy who seemed overburdened by the thought of handling 'all things alone' during peak hours but could not say so to his superior.

'Yes sure.' He replied as tersely as he could and left the table.

40

In another area of the same resort Montu was grilling the Asst. Manager - Banquets. He was fairing very badly though. 'So, you can't give me details regarding the full occupancy in the next fortnight or so and who all are booking the rooms?' Montu asked looking pissed off and ready to box the fellow.

'Sir, hotel policy. I cannot give you those details. Sir you can give me your dates, and I can find out whether the requested rooms and the banquet halls are available on those dates. But I really cannot give you the complete details about our hotel booking,' replied a completely irritated Ajay. He had had a major argument with his wife before leaving for office regarding the most important question of the morning – Who would be making the bed-tea? He lost pathetically and had to finally make the tea. Consequently he was late for work and got a run-down on hotel rules by his senior.

To top it all, the first client of the day was grilling him as if he was the owner of the resort. *Banging his head on the wall would be better than arguing with the bloke,* he thought to himself. But he had a job to do. And the booking, if it did finally manage to come through would take his sales targets to delightful levels. *I cannot give up now. Come on Ajay behave like an ass with an ass.* The fresh Masters in Business Administration guy for whom it was the first job after his recently concluded honeymoon, told himself quietly.

'Okay...can you leave me alone for sometime? I will just see the place once again, and then will join you at the reception,' Montu gritted his teeth to maintain his cool as he said this. 'Okay sir,' said the unabashed Ajay. 'Just ask the receptionist to buzz me once you are done with your inspection.' (He wanted to add 'snooping around' but refrained himself.) He might punch me anytime now. *It is better I leave him alone for a while to cool down.* The sensible Ajay gave a nod and went away. 'Oh and please do check up all the alternate dates as I had asked you to earlier,' Montu added. Ajay nodded silently and went away.

Ritesh had given Montu the dates which had to be checked. This was crucial information and Montu did not want to fail him. This way they could plan out the best day for meeting Chabra. They wanted it to be one of the busiest days so that no one would notice them while gaining information about his operations in the resort as well as in Delhi. Ritesh had told him that Chabra would not go in for a property in Shimla for the simple reason of owning a resort property, unless there was some other motive behind it.

He checked the resort grounds thoroughly to his satisfaction and asked short, well-framed questions regarding the various entries and exit points. He gathered information regarding the owner from the odd and unsuspecting housekeeper, the severely tired and grumbling chef who had just been relieved after finishing a double, day-and-night shift and even a chatty old guard at the back-door having his *beedi*. Montu forked out some important pieces of information that he knew would hugely please Ritesh.

Finally he went upto the reception desk and asked the same girl who was busy chatting with her other colleague, if he could meet Mr Ajay Guleria again. Ajay came strolling in after five minutes. He had the information but did not want to show that he would comply with the request easily.

'So sir, are you satisfied with the layout and all?' he enquired with a tight, tolerant smile. 'Oh yes. Beautiful. All good. I just need you to tell me if the dates I mentioned are free for booking or not,' Montu, quite proud of his sleuthing skills replied happily 'Sir almost all the dates you have mentioned are full. But if you are really interested, we can adjust something for you.'

'How is that??' Montu, quite new to the whole experience of booking banquet parties and hotel rooms, asked sounding puzzled. 'Sir, some of them have tentatively booked but have not payed the advance. If you can pay it, we will book it for you instead. You see first-come-first-serve,' Ajay explained patiently with a smile.

'Oh okay, if that is the case, do give me the list. I will consult the other family members and get back to you tomorrow morning.' Montu handled the most important answer which had been drummed into him by Ritesh well and proper.

'Hmmm...sir the sooner you get back to us the better,' Ajay stressed, a bit dejected at being unable to close the sale immediately. 'Yes, of course. Sure. I understand,' Montu babbled. Ajay handed Montu the important piece of paper, with the latter refusing to take his eyes away from it till it was safely in his custody. Triumphant at last, Montu gave a broad grin to the banquet manager. He shook hands excitedly before leaving a very puzzled Ajay.

'So how was it?' Ritesh asked as soon as he entered the hotel room which Montu and he were sharing, looking slightly drunk and very excited.

'Oh you are back.' Montu who was busy surfing the channels and at the same time singing an odd tune, looked up and found his friend trying to bolt the room door but being unstable on his feet, missing it several times.

'Shall I help?' Montu offered.

'No thank you, I got it,' replied Ritesh a bit irritated. 'But never leave the door ajar, even when you are alone okay?' he said once he had managed to bolt it finally. 'Self-security should be our prime concern always,' he further elaborated.

'Okay sorry. I will remember that,' Montu apologised looking glum.

'Hmm...so how did it go for you? Were you able to get some information on our Delhi friend and his state of health?' Ritesh asked Montu curious to know whether he had been able to fulfil his part of the job well or not. A lot depended on that. Of course, even he had sufficient information on him. But if Montu can substantiate that, then it would be even better. Ritesh thought to himself as he impatiently waited for Montu to answer.

'Yes, yes, of course. I have a lot to tell you,' Montu said cheerfully.

'Firstly, no doubt our man is loaded with money. He bought the resort three years back. And rumours are there were other powerful bidders. You know, local bidders who wanted the property but he bid the highest and payed almost all the money upfront. One of the drivers passed on this information to the young housekeeper I happened to interact with. He was generally boasting about how rich and powerful his current boss is. The property was sold for more than sixteen crores and another crore or so have been spent on it for some renovation work,' Montu gushed on happily.

'Wow Montu I am really impressed. You do have some good information here, which I already knew but have been reconfirmed by your findings quite well.'

'Secondly, there is some funny, side business going on in the resort. One of the old chefs told me that whenever he works at night, he can hear noises, like trucks or some heavy vehicles coming inside the resort property and downloading stuff. He swore that once he even saw Mr K. Chabra and a few of his personal aides, personally go for a night walk towards the woods, adjacent to the resort. Now why would he want to do that in the middle of the night? It seems that even the police and a few top politicians of the state are involved in this deal.' Montu winked at Ritesh, who was himself smiling. 'The old guard also confirmed this for a pack of Marlburo cigarettes. I had just said that it is quite noisy at night whereas this place is supposed to be peaceful, that is when he gave it out.' Montu boasted about his manoeuvring skills.

'And thirdly and most importantly, I have the list of dates on which the resort will be heavily booked. And luckily we also have the dates when the film crew is coming. They have booked almost the complete resort. And it seems we will have many foreigners staying at the resort at the same time. There are many outdoor as well as indoor events happening at that time. Though, many of them still need to be confirmed as per the banquet's Asst. Manager.' Montu finished his round with the ace.

'Very well done Montu. You are pretty good. You have fared better than I thought. I am really happy,' Ritesh praised his friend wholeheartedly. He had got the correct information and even valuable add-ons which would greatly benefit his own theory.

'I think from what you have told me and from what all I have found out today, Chabra is doing much better than before. He has developed his networks even more and has obviously got richer over the years. I even came to know that his links in the present govt are pretty strong. People, many big shots and rich men, come here to Shimla either to meet him or just to get their jobs done, to get tenders passed or for leisure and all and for which of course he charges hefty sums unless he wants to bribe some of them. And he does that too. It is also certain that he holds secret parties, I guess these are rave parties for his exclusive clients, including foreigners, mostly held in the nearby jungles and sometimes even inside the resort property. That place is perfect for such things,' Ritesh ended looking excited.

'Anyways, now we have to wait for his call. He will call me soon. But we will go the day after the the film crew has checked in and have one of their parties going on. I suspect there are more things going on there than what is visible to the naked eye. We can maybe come to know a bit more if we spend a good part of the night there. I will try for a late-evening appointment only so that we can stay over afterwards and have some of our own fun too.' Ritesh disclosed his plan to an ever-nodding Montu, who listened and nodded as if he had a spring fitted on his neck.

'But all this needs to be carefully planned. And of course we will have to check the list to see the confirmed parties of the movie crew. Chabra had mentioned he would be personally overseeing those parties. So now you know why this list is so important,' Ritesh clarified, waving the piece of paper in front of Montu, who nodded once again.

41

'Hey wake up sleepy head. We need to get ready by 7:30 am.'

'Mmm...don't disturb me Deep.' Aparajita snuggled further inside her fluffy quilt.

'Don't you want to see Kufri?' Deepanita smiled and said the words. No response.

'Aupora we are all going to Kufri today. It is drizzling though. But I guess that will not deter our over-zealous, "want to see it all" group.' Deepanita laughed. No response. 'Don't you want to come?' Deepanita repeated patiently.

Suddenly the words rang a bell and Aparajita, stirred and stretched. 'What? Is it today? I thought it was for tomorrow.'

'No darling it was all planned for today.'

'Now hurry up.' Deepanita did not lose anytime to further drive in the point.

'Oh okay okay, you are just like my mother. Always after me! But I love you,' Aparajita got up and smiled at her best friend.

'There is a bon-fire at the hotel tomorrow night.'

'Wow, looking forward to it. But won't we be too tired?' Deep and Aupora found two of their girlfriends talking to each other as they joined them for breakfast.

'Hi, had a good sleep?' Deepanita asked the two. 'Oh yes, very nice. I just love to go to bed here but the problem is once I get under the blanket I just don't want to come out,' replied Indrani through her clattering teeth. Everyone laughed with her at that and completely agreed. The girls quickly finished their breakfasts and got ready for their bus ride to Kufri.

'I think I will soon look like an apple,' joked Aniket taking in the fresh air. Aparajita who was sitting beside him in the bus which their group had hired for the day, laughed out loud. 'You are so funny,' she said after a while.

'Am I?' Aniket smiled feeling pleased. She had kept her word by never leaving him by himself. And he felt on top of the moon to be with her (and Deepanita) for the whole time.

'You know, you should always smile. You look your best when you do that. Besides, others around you feel happy too,' Aniket told her giving her one of his own.

'Hmm...that means you will smile every time I smile, right? Right?' Aparajita mocked him. 'Yes. Right,' Aniket said simply. 'You are such a sweet heart Aniket,' Aparajita felt touched and replied.

'Am I really?' Aniket looked at her seriously and asked. Aparajita, a bit puzzled by the question and her own reaction to it, quickly looked away. 'Oh you know what I mean...' she mumbled quietly. Aniket wanted to say something more but the moment was lost as everyone started to play *antakshari*.

To everybody's joy the tiny hill station – Kufri turned out to be as expected – fresh and indescribably beautiful. The group was spellbound by its supreme beauty – lofty snow peaks, lush green valleys, enchanting mountain lakes, ancient and beautifully structured temples and monasteries...and amongst it all happy and smiling faces. It was all so heavenly.

But it was not so for Siddharth. He was strangely feeling very sad. He had nobody whom he could call his friend. Even the people supposedly closest to him – his parents were distant figures to him. This place made him even lonelier. Just then his eyes fell on the threesome who always stuck together. He envied them. *Why can't I have friends like them?* he thought. He kept staring at their silly attempts of throwing the handmade snowballs at each other and then squealing with complete delight when one was hit – as if they were toddlers. Deepanita was laughing away, looking completely happy and at peace with herself. *Maybe I should go down to them and say hello. But, I don't think it is a good idea. They might get shocked or may not even acknowledge my presence, let alone greet me.* He checked himself, thought better of it and turned direction towards the woods.

'Aniket, let's check out the forest area and collect some hard pine cones as mementos,' Aparajita suggested. Aniket agreed wholeheartedly but needed a warm drink to get started. 'But before that let me go and get some coffee for us,' he offered. 'Okay while you get those...Deepanita and I will go ahead. You can follow us with the coffee. Is that okay?' Aparajita suggested. 'Hmm...okay, but walk slowly. I will join you guys soon.' Deepanita who was a few steps away hadn't heard this bit. Aparajita waved at her and pointed towards the woods. Deepanita nodded back. Both the girls started walking towards the thick forest.

Siddharth who was lost in thought smoking a cigarette suddenly heard Ritesh talking to Montu. Something inside him told him not to move and so he stayed glued to his spot. Both were unaware of his presence. The trees were a good camouflage for him.

'So when do you think Chabra will call?' Montu was asking Ritesh. 'I don't know. I guess he must be in Shimla by now,' Ritesh replied seriously. 'We need to be very careful. He is a well-connected guy and one wrong move by us might get us into a lot of trouble,' Ritesh warned his friend. 'But we are his suppliers. Why should he feel threatened by us?' Montu asked puzzled. 'Stupid, we are not anything to him yet. And don't forget we are asking around and digging things about him. He might feel offended,' Ritesh informed impatiently. 'He knows our *maal* is of good and pure quality and I guess he needs it, otherwise he would have never agreed to meet me so easily.'

So they are here in Shimla to do some kind of a deal with this Chabra fellow. And I thought Ritesh loves nature so much that he did not want to miss this trip, Siddharth thought to himself.

'Hi,' said a voice from behind. Aniket was looking at him, a polite smile on his face. Siddharth jumped. But collecting himself said, 'Oh...hello Aniket!' Aniket had not forgiven Siddharth for almost breaking up his friendship with Aparajita, but he was in no mood to fight or create an unpleasant scene. He hadn't expected him. Siddharth saw that Aniket looked uneasy and the other two inseparables were standing at a distance, glaring at him. Siddharth waved at them and smiled. Both ignored it completely and instead called out to Aniket, 'Come on Aniket!'

Unfazed, Siddharth turned to Aniket and asked, 'How are you buddy?' He wanted to be friends with him. He had found him to be an honest and caring boy out of the whole lot he knew. None in his class were worth making good friends with, even though he did hang out with them once in a while. But Aniket – shy, intelligent, funny and dependable had something in him that made him very likable. But he also knew that Aniket was upset with him for damaging his relationship with Aparajita. Though as of now it seemed that things were all right.

'I am good. What are you doing out here, all alone?' he heard Aniket asking him a little suspiciously. 'Me, oh just the thing you are doing, taking a closer look at Mother Nature. Ha ha ha ha,' Siddharth informed laughing.

Ritesh called out to them on hearing his throaty laughter, 'Hey you two, what are you guys doing here?' Siddharth looked at Aniket and laughed again. Aniket only smiled at that. The girls called out to Aniket again.

Not wanting to join Ritesh and Montu, Aniket quickly bade good bye to Siddharth, 'Oh I gotta go, but you carry on.' 'Oh. Why?' Sidhharth asked mocking him. No response. 'Come on Aniket! Let the girls be for a while. Or ask them to join us,' Siddharth suggested gently. 'No thank you.' 'You all carry on. I have to go,' Aniket put in firmly. 'Anyway you have managed to damage our friendship quite well. I have not forgiven you for that,' Aniket told him bitterly before moving away. He could not help it. The words just tumbled out.

'About that…I am really sorry. Believe me. If Aparajita had not bugged me so much I would have not done this at all. But she really did hurt me where it hurts the most. I will not forgive her for that either. But anyways let bygones be bygones,' Siddharth smiled weakly and tried to explain his side of the story. He would have gone on but was interrupted by Ritesh. 'Hey Sid, come and join us,' Ritesh was calling out to him. 'Yeah, coming,' he said disappointed. He was envious of Aniket who was walking back to where his good friends were waiting for him patiently. Siddharth on the other hand joined the impatient rogues.

42

When Aniket returned, the girls scowled at him for taking so long, but eventually understood. After walking with them for a while, Deepanita made an excuse to go a little ahead of them to take a look at some wild flowers. 'You both can come at your own pace,' she said mysteriously, looking at Aniket. Aniket got the hint. He loved her for that. She was always sweet and helpful. 'Don't go too far off,' Aparajita warned her, a little concerned. 'Okay!' Deepanita replied without looking back.

She felt the dull ache in her heart sharpen. *If Aniket expresses his love for Aparajita and she accepts him, this will be 'the end' to my own dreams…but if they do love each other and I am wrong, then it must happen.*

Deep in her own thoughts she did not realise that due to the fresh rains earlier in the morning, the melting snow had become more slippery. Suddenly her foot slipped and she fell down, twisting her ankle badly. She cried out loud at the pain it caused. But it did not get her the necessary reaction she was expecting. *I might have left the two much behind me.* She tried to get up. But the sharp pain was too much to bear and she sat down, tears of frustration and pain running down uncontrollably. She kept sitting unable to move thinking what best to do under the circumstances. She was starting to feel worried as it was getting dark and she could neither hear nor see her friends. Just then, she heard the rustling of leaves and turned her face towards the direction of the sound.

'Hey don't move,' said the strong, gentle voice from behind the trees. She knew the voice minus the gentleness. Fearing the worst, she turned towards the direction of the voice, still sitting. It indeed was Siddharth. Not knowing what to say, she said the first thing that came to her mind, 'I...I...twisted my ankle.' She wanted to sound matter-of-fact but her voice deceived her. It came out weak and small. Siddharth came to her and sat down on his haunches. She had already removed her shoes and socks to estimate the damage. Siddharth held her injured leg in his hands to take a better look at it. Despite wearing so much of clothing and thick woollens, Deepanita felt an electric current run through her at his first touch. It intensified a thousand times when his face came closer to take a better look at the damage. She tried to recoil but he was holding her firmly. 'Don't move,' he ordered firmly. 'Oh, you have a cut too. We will have to carry you back,' Siddharth explained softly, noting Deepanita's discomfiture. 'No...no...I am fine. I just need a stick or something to walk with,' she blabbered, terrified at being carried by her friend's enemy, *her enemy.*

In Pursuit of Ecstasy • 159

Siddharth looked at her then, full on the face. 'Look I know you don't like me. But believe me, if I do not carry you, you won't be able to walk. Your friends are nowhere in sight. It is getting dark. And this is the most practical thing to do. Okay?' Siddharth finished in one breath.

He felt a strong urge to kiss this silly and stubborn girl and knock some sense back into her. But he knew that would be the most unwise thing to do. She would go into her cocoon further and the dislike will turn into hatred. And he wanted the exact opposite to happen. He really wanted her to trust him and come close to him...*like no one else had*. Shaking his thoughts off for the moment, he tried to coax her gently. 'I really won't eat you...you know?' he smiled gently.

'Uh...huh...I guess...you are right,' Deepanita answered feeling confused and weak. 'Will you be able to carry me till there?' she asked a little nervously. Siddharth laughed out loud. *God! He's so handsome.*

'Of course, yes,' he said still smiling as he picked her up in his arms. *Oh how I wish she stays like this in my arms...safe and secure.* And then he scolded himself for straying for the umpteenth time.

In another part of the forest, Aniket and Aparajita were talking. No, Aniket was almost pleading and Aparajita was listening in amazement and shock. 'Please Aupora, it has always been like this. From the time I met you. I knew it.' 'But how is it possible Aniket? I mean, we are friends, best friends!' she said trying to make sense of it all.

'Yes, we are and will always be. But who says that that we cannot be...errr...boyfriend...and girlfriend? I love you...with all my heart,' he tried to reason out with her.

'But I thought that Deepanita and you…I mean…I thought you liked her and she…' she left the sentence midway. She looked so confused that Aniket did not know how to bring her back to her cheerful self.

'Hey…ha haha ha…I really got you there,' Aniket faked his laugh. 'I was just joking man. Just joking. Really. Don't look so sad. And anyways I am not so bad for a boyfriend am I?' He asked after a brief pause, half in zest and half serious.

'*Aniket!!* Don't do such things,' Aparajita replied, still confused and angry with him. 'This is not funny,' saying so, she boxed him on his back. 'Aww!…ok…ok…sorry!! Forgive me now and smile,' Aniket requested pretending to be in pain.

She just mumbled her consent and started walking a little ahead of him. She felt a restlessness she had not felt earlier. *Why did he joke with me like that? He looked so serious? I wonder.*

'It is getting dark. Let us go back now,' a concerned Aniket broke into her topsy-turvy thoughts. 'Hmm', she said and followed him out. 'I hope Deepanita has gone back,' Aniket said out aloud. He was also feeling guilty for not going after his friend to check on her. But he knew Deepanita was sensible that way and would find her way back.

Back at their holiday resort, Aniket and Aparajita started looking around for Deepanita. Unsuccessful in locating her they got worried. 'What do we do now?' said a very worried Aparajita. 'Don't worry, we will go out again and look for her,' replied an equally worried and terribly guilty Aniket. He went to the centre of the hall where all the students had collected and announced loudly – 'Okay listen up friends. Deepanita is missing. She was with us. But she decided to go ahead of us after a while. We thought she would come back on her own

But she is not here. We are slightly worried. I think we should go and look for her.' He finished loud and strong.

'Yes...definitely' murmured several voices. The professors amongst the students also joined in and asked them about her last whereabouts. 'Take a few torches,' one of the girls suggested. 'Yes and the first-aid kit too. You know just in case ...' said another worried voice. Aparajita was really worried now. Aniket tried his best to console her. 'Don't worry Aupora. She is a strong and smart girl. Nothing will happen. Let's wait.' He soothed her. Aparajita felt glad for his strong presence by her side then.

Unaware of all this, Siddharth walked in carrying Deepanita in his arms. She had wanted to get down as they neared the hall area. But he refused to listen to her. 'Come on Deep...don't be a child. Stay where you are. The cut looks bad, you can hardly bear the pain and can in no way walk...just yet. You need proper care first.' He said firmly without noticing that due to his concern he had called her by the name that only her friends addressed her by. Deepanita caught that. She blushed and stopped fighting him. Not only was she tired, she was completely confused with her responses to him.

Taking in the scene now, he understood. People were missing them or at least Deepanita, courtesy, her two loyal friends. 'Oh...there she is...with Siddharth,' said a voice. All turned around then. 'Sid what happened?' some of his classmates asked. Aparajita rushed towards her. 'Deep! Deep! What happened baby?' she ignored Siddharth completely. Siddharth put her down gently on the sofa and quickly asked for a chair for her leg. Indrani passed him the chair. Aparajita looked as if she was about to cry. Deepanita just smiled at all those who surrounded her and said softly, 'I am fine now. Had slipped and twisted my ankle. Thankfully Siddharth was nearby and got an air-lift,' she tried to joke. Others smiled. Siddharth got a lot of pats on his back. 'Good job boy,' said the relieved professors.

The local doctor was also called in by then. The group left for Shimla, after everything had been taken care of well and proper. Deepanita had been given a painkiller. The damage to her ankle was not as bad as it looked. The doctor assured her that she would be up and walking in a couple of days. He prescribed a few painkillers and an ointment for her and asked her not to move around much for a couple of days.

Siddharth moved away once things were in control again. Her friends were all fussing over her. And he did not want to join the party. He wanted her alone – all for himself. But Aparajita was still his enemy. He still wanted 'Ms Snooty' to learn her lesson. He had still not forgiven her for the way she had insulted him in front of someone whom he considered to be his biggest enemy.

'Who is it? ' asked a sleepy Ritesh. He looked at the time automatically as he answered his mobile. It was 10:30 pm at night. *Who will call up so late?* He thought to himself. The displayed number was not familiar. 'Hello Ritesh, this is Chabra here.' Ritesh sat bolt upright on his bed then. 'Oh…Hello Mr Chabra. Sorry I was sleeping.' He answered all alert now. At the same time he spread the piece of paper Montu had got from the resort.

'No…no…it is okay. Actually I am calling in late. Ha ha ha ha.' He heard Chabra laugh on the other side, though did not get the joke himself. 'So you can come and meet me tomorrow evening – 7:30 pm. Okay?' he asked.

Ritesh quickly looked into the paper to check if it was a good date for executing his personal plans too. Then brightening up, he answered, 'Tomorrow evening is perfect Mr Chabra.' 'Hmm…good…good…then see you tomorrow. And I have a big event at the resort, so we will make it quick. Be on time,' Chabra informed him. 'Okay. Sure. Will be there at the said time,' Ritesh answered happily. Keeping the phone down he woke up Montu who had gone off to sleep too. Tomorrow is our D-day. 'Sorry?' asked a confused and groggy Montu. 'Tomorrow we are going to the party at Lord's Holiday Manor,' Ritesh smiled triumphantly and informed Montu. 'Oh okay,' the light of knowledge dawned on the hugely tired and sleepy boy; he gave a small smile and promptly went to bed again.

'Come on. Hurry up. We need to be out before any of the others come out of their rooms. If those guys notice us, we will have to make an appearance at the stupid bonfire party. Otherwise they will get suspicious.' Ritesh looked outside his hotel room window and urged Montu at the same time to get ready fast.

Dusk was fast approaching. The valley looked washed and fresh after the day's rainfall. Standing by the window taking in the freshness even Ritesh felt confident, excited and nervous all at the same time for the evening. The whole morning Montu and he had planned how they would go about the whole thing. Since they had visited and seen the resort earlier, he was confident that they would pull through. Yet there was a nagging doubt. And it was troubling him even now.

'I should have spoken to Siddharth and taken him into confidence. We do need a third guy to back us up. But he seems so distant and cold that I could not muster the courage to share our purpose of this trip to Shimla,' Ritesh shared.

'...After all, we do have to be very careful and besides, I never found him to be interested in our work.' He was chatting with Montu but it seemed he was trying to convince himself.

Ritesh had always wanted Siddharth in his gang as his second-in-command. Had even cajoled and coaxed him to be a part of it. But Siddharth had just shown polite interest. He would hang out with them, he knew about their work and all, was good enough to keep everything about them to himself. But never tried to help them or act as a part of the gang. He would buy the *'stuff'* for personal consumption from them once in a while but that was it. No questions asked. Never. This puzzled Ritesh a lot. But he respected, admired and even feared Siddharth, enough to leave him alone.

'As of now we really do need a third person. And Siddharth is the only one I can think of. He would not only be best for the job but would also be completely reliable,' Ritesh said.

'Why don't you ask for his help?' Montu asked. 'You don't have to give him the intricate details. Just tell him you need his help to keep a watch for us. In case we do not turn up by say 11:00 pm, he can call in the local police to look out for us at the Lord's Holiday resort,' Montu suggested.

'Hmmm...you are right. I guess he won't refuse us for this much help. Besides he is not the snoopy and chatty kinds,' Ritesh concluded.

'Thanks buddy. You are turning out to be a big help,' Ritesh smiled at his friend looking much relieved.

43

Lying on his bed Siddharth was trying to decide whether or not to go for the bonfire. He did not feel like partying much. But he knew Deepanita and her friends would be there for sure. *Ankle sprain or no sprain. Deepanita would not want to miss out on all the fun.* He just knew. *Besides she must have rested the whole day. It had been raining throughout the day; they could not have gone out anyways with her bad leg and an equally bad weather. I must go and see how she is doing.* He thought to himself as he got up to get ready, feeling responsible for her somehow.

'Hey Sid, you in there buddy?' Siddharth heard a voice call out to him from outside his room, as he was coming out of the bathroom. *What does Ritesh want?* Siddharth, recognising the voice thought to himself.

'Hi. Busy?' Ritesh poked in his head and asked as soon as Siddharth opened the door. 'No not much,' Siddharth answered him cautiously. Though he did hang out with Ritesh and his friends once in a while, he did not feel any special kind of affinity towards them. In fact, he clearly knew their intentions and what they wanted from him. He was a good client and could get them richer and loaded clients like himself. But he did not mind this fact. The arrangement suited him fine. So he tried to maintain a relationship good enough to get him by. He did need his cigarettes once in a while and Ritesh never asked for immediate payments. And Siddharth on his part never took advantage of the fact. It was a good working relationship between the two parties.

'So, can I come in for a moment?' Ritesh enquired smiling. 'Yeah sure,' Siddharth answered him warily.

'Hmm...nice room,' Ritesh said looking around the room brightly. 'Is it?' Siddharth asked him sardonically. He knew there was not much difference between Ritesh and his room. 'I mean all the rooms here are nice. Isn't it?' Ritesh corrected himself. The fellow has something up his sleeve, Siddharth guessed.

'Sid, actually I have come for a favour,' Ritesh came to the point now. 'A big favour. And you are the only person who can help me with this.' 'What is it Ritesh?' Siddharth asked curious.

'Well, you see, Montu and I are here on a special mission. We came on this trip not because we wanted to see Shimla or wanted to chill and stuff, we came for a very specific purpose. There is someone we are meeting...for our business...err...you understand?' He looked at Siddharth knowingly.

'Hmm...so?' Siddharth nodded in understanding and urged him to continue.

'So this person is quite a powerful man in our line of business, but still we want to be pretty sure that if we do business with him, we will be secure and trouble free,' Ritesh said and his nervous excitement showing through.

'Now, he has called us to meet him tonight. We are going there. What I just want from you is to keep a watch for us,' Ritesh said the words slowly, as if waiting for Siddharth to protest. But on getting no response he continued.

'You know, just make sure you contact the local police if we do not return by 11:00 pm or so and come to this address. And contact Mr K. Chabra the owner of the resort property.' He handed Siddharth the piece of paper on which the address was given.

Siddharth realised that this was the same Chabra Ritesh had mentioned in Kufri when he had eavesdropped on Montu and him. '…Just this much. That is all.' He tried to coax and at the same time play the whole thing down.

'I am sure there is nothing to worry about. But in our line of business, we must be prepared at all times.' Ritesh ended not sure whether this moody fellow will accept his request or not.

'Hmm…' Siddharth considered the request. This was nothing major. He could handle it. And besides, they were his classmates and his friends in some way. He could do this much for them. All these thoughts were hovering one after the other in his mind. Siddharth kept quiet for a long time, assessing the pros and cons of the request. Ritesh became a little apprehensive that Siddharth would refuse him.

'So?' He broke the silence impatient to get an answer.

'Okay. I will do it for you. But do be careful. And once you reach the place, give me a buzz. So that I know for sure that you both are in the resort. Okay?' Siddharth broke his silence with a word of caution.

'Okay sure. It is a good idea. Thanks a lot buddy.' Ritesh smiled with relief.

'Don't mention it. But remember, I will not repeat it,' Siddharth told him pointedly.

'Of course. I owe you one for this. Okay. Bye then. See you soon,' Ritesh beamed at his confidant gratefully and left.

The party had already begun by the time Siddharth reached the place. The weather was quite chilly and Siddharth found everyone huddled around the huge bonfire – singing, talking, eating and making merry. Siddharth took in the sight rather reluctantly. He wanted to be alone. Alone with…He quickly dismissed the thoughts and joined the group. 'Hey Sid, we are playing "truth or dare". Come and join us,' informed one of his classmates good humouredly. 'Okay,' Siddharth smiled in acknowledgement. '…But no thanks. I am all right. Will just watch you guys,' he replied after a brief pause as his eyes scanned the crowd for the pair of eyes he so desperately wanted to see. But they were nowhere in sight.

He spotted the other two sitting comfortably besides each other laughing and talking intimately about something. Aniket had a beer bottle in his hand and was already slightly drunk. Even the girl was drinking. *Poor thing does not know that her 'Mr Hero' has a fetish for the bottle.* Siddharth thought to himself as he recalled the day when he had got Aniket drunk purposely to find out information about Aparajita. But he had got so drunk that he had puked. That had saved Aparajita. Siddharth thought sardonically. *She should be careful with him.* But immediately his thoughts changed track, *how could they leave Deepanita all alone?* He though angrily as he prepared to walk up to them. *She is always so concerned for Aparajita and look at her so-called best friend, not the least bothered about her dear friend.* His anger was rising by the minute.

'Hey!' he said, as he reached them, controlling his urge to give them a good lecture on what is expected out of true friends in times of real need – like now.

'How are you guys?' he asked as both looked up in surprise. Since when did the fox decide to say hello to its prey? Aparajita thought. Deepanita had a lot to do with this change. But this was not going to be permanent. Aparajita mused with complete conviction.

'Oh...hi' responded an unsure and a bit tipsy Aniket for both Aparajita and himself. An awkward silence followed. None wanted to break it.

Siddharth finally blurted out, 'Look, I do not want to disturb you guys...just generally wanted to know, how is your friend?' Siddharth stressed on the last two words.

'She is very well thank you!' This time it was Aparajita who answered back, in a tone that conveyed in no uncertain terms – Go away we do not need you.

'Thank you for taking care of her today. But I guess we will be okay from here on. You don't need to bother,' she stung back. She suspected that the scheming boy was up to something. Maybe *'divide–and–take– out–secrets'* the way he did, with Aniket. She wanted to keep her innocent friend as much away from him as possible.

'Look Aparajita, I know we don't like each other. But I really am not here to fight with any of you. I am just concerned.' Siddharth came to the point.

'...She had a pretty bad fall. Though she is taking it all bravely, the doctor separately told me not let her move much, for at least 2-3 days. Now that both of you are here, I was wondering whether she would be okay on her own?' There! it all came tumbling out. All the things he wanted to keep to himself. But there was no way that this 'Ms Snooty' was going to let him see her. He felt frustrated and very upset with her.

Both her friends looked up at Siddharth as if the cat had got their tongue. What had caused the change of heart was something neither Aparajita nor Aniket were able to comprehend. They were really puzzled.

'Look I just want to go and say hello to her once. Is that such a huge problem? I can even check on her while I am there,' Siddharth offered gently. 'And I won't take out any secrets from her. Promise.' He smiled and looked at Aparajita desperately wanting her to believe him. Aparajita was taken in by his earnestness and frank acceptance of the fact that he knew she suspected him.

'Hmm...okay...she is reading a book in the room. Our room no. is 32 A. Since you are the saviour, I guess there is no harm in your going and checking on her. And maybe she needs something or the other. I will go in a while. But Aniket and I are the coordinators for tonight's event so our presence here is also important,' Aparajita replied cautiously.

'Okay thanks,' Siddharth replied, feeling guilty for having thought of them as being the worst of friends.

44

'Come in,' Deepanita replied, thinking it must be Aniket coming in to check on her. She was a little worried for him. After the fall she did not get ample time to ask him about his success with Aparajita. Neither did any of them say anything. She had an idea about his drinkning habits though she had never confronted him regarding it nor had she disclosed this fact to anyone. Not even Aparajita. But tonight she knew she was not there and Aparajita was alone with him. Anything could happen. She thought feeling a bit anxious.

Deepanita was sitting on her bed with her back resting against the propped-up pillows, sprained leg outstretched besides the good leg which was partially covered with a quilt. She was holding a thriller book but her thoughts were with her friends. So she gave a start when the tall and well-built figure that walked in a little cautiously and said, 'Hi Deepanita. I hope you are doing well?' It was a question laced with concern, Siddharth looked at the girl whose lovely face was etched in his mind and refused to fade away. *I must be the last person she might be expecting,* he thought. As her confused eyes met his, he smiled, his heart beating so fast as if he were running a hundred-metre sprint.

'Uh...huh...*You??* What are you doing here?' the confused girl asked, without realising she sounded more accusing than greeting the guest.

There was a long uncomfortable silence, during which Deepanita's mind was busy trying to get some answers to the volley of questions which raced through her mind. *Why is he here? Who sent him? Does he mean to harm me now? Does he want to take advantage of my state and twist out information about Aparajita? Why is he looking at me as if he is really concerned about me??*

'Oh, don't look so upset. You see...I just came to...just to see if you are okay. After all I did find you first. And it is my responsibility to at least check on you and find out if things are okay.' He correctly read Deepanita's expression and tried to ease her fears.

'No...no...I thought it was Aniket. He was supposed to come and check on me,' Deepanita lied. 'Why don't you pull up a chair and sit down?' She smiled weakly and tried to make amends for her bad behaviour.

'So? How is the pain?' Siddharth asked her as his large frame tried to make itself comfortable on the 'not so large' study chair. 'Oh okay. Just that I can't move. Aupora and Aniket have made sure that I don't,' she tried to joke. Siddharth just smiled at that. Deepanita suddenly realised it was not a very pleasant topic for Siddharth whose dislike for her friend had been more than apparent in the recent past.

'Siddharth I am really thankful to you. If you would not have been there, I don't know what might have happened. Deepanita shuddered as she remembered the place – cold, dark and deep inside the forest. It might have been quite difficult for her to walk out into the open on her own. Siddharth's presence had really been a blessing. Siddharth looked at the passing expressions on her face from one of fear to relief. He wanted to hug her tightly and tell her nothing would harm her as long as he was there. *But was he there?? They were not even friends.* This thought brought him back to reality. 'Oh don't worry Deep, it was nothing. After all, what are friends for?' It was already out before he could stop it. 'Err...I mean college mates. I might be mean to you again once you go back to college. But it was my responsibility as your senior to bring you back to safety. Anyone would have done what I did.' He corrected himself a little embarrassed.

Deepanita was touched. She knew that this boy would seldom go out of his way to help Aparajita or her. But he had. She knew he had been very hurt when Aparajita had rebuked him and had reported his misdemeanour to his father in front of the whole college. But still he had helped her. And now he had even come to see if she was doing okay. After all, the 'brute' had a heart. She smiled unconsciously. 'Hmm...you find something funny?' Siddharth asked looking at her, smiling. Her smile was irresistible, he found himself addicted to it. 'No...no...just like that,' Deepanita said a little embarrassed.

'Okay, so now that you are comfortable and smiling away...for some odd reason, I will leave you in peace. Take care and get well soon.' He smiled and teased her, then just before he was about to go he noticed the quilt was not covering her legs properly so he bent down automatically to pull it and put it over her. In doing so his hands touched hers. An electric current passed through him. And he saw that even Deepanita jerked away her hands quickly. This was an odd feeling. He pulled his hands away.

'Thanks Siddharth,' he heard Deepanita say a little awkwardly. When he looked up, she was smiling the same infectious smile. He mumbled a quick 'Goodnight' and went away as quietly as he had walked into her room, leaving a very puzzled Deepanita behind.

'Au...pora. . .' Aniket now on his sixth bottle looked at his equally drunk best friend and said feeling bold, 'I have a confession to make.' 'You do? How many confessions do you have in toto? And b.t.w. if it is it like the one you had in Kufri, then fool the other girls. I am not going to fall for it this time,' Aupora replied, teasing him and totally unconcerned. She was having a good time. Enjoying the drink, the food, music, the bonfire, in fact she was enjoying it all – the complete freedom to be herself without worrying too much about what time it was and what lie she would have to cook up for her parents for staying out so long and then coming back drunk.

Drunk – that was an unimaginable word in the 'Mukherjee' household. Her father loathed people who were addicted to the bottle even those who socially drank. Aparajita liked drinking with friends once in a while. But she never could do it freely for fear that her father might come to know of it and throw her out of the house.

But tonight, she was not only enjoying her beer but thoroughly enjoying Aniket's company too. It was after a long time that they were like this together – comfortable and easy in each other's company. She had forgotten how entertaining and funny he could be. His funny gestures and jokes always made her laugh, however sad or upset she would be. And he was so protective about her. And moreover, she just loved the feeling of getting all his attention throughout the trip till now. Because of the fight between them, she had all but forgotten how nice it felt to be pampered by him. And also it was only because of him that his mom had actually allowed her to come for the trip so easily. He was a darling. She wanted to thank him. But she did not know how to thank her best friend without sounding too formal or superfluous. So she waited for the right time.

'Aupora…' Aniket broke into her merry thoughts. 'I seriously have a confession,' Aniket informed her as soberly as he could. 'Okay tell you what. I too have a confession. So you tell me yours then I will tell you mine okay?' Aupora suggested happily. 'Hmmm…okay…fine,' Aniket adjusted his glasses and replied, feeling clueless about what Aparajita might want to share with him. But he was sure that Aparajita might not be in the frame of mind to make her confessions after he had made his. The thought made him a little nervous.

But I have to do this. Even Deepanita is not here today. 'I love you Aupora,' he said turning her towards him and holding both her hands in his. She was smiling and as always looking gorgeous. 'What?' She tried to hear his words, someone had started strumming the guitar and the others were clapping. Aniket's voice drowned. 'I said, I love you…I always have… but never told you,' he said it all in one go, this time loud enough for even others standing nearby to hear his confession. The sudden stillness in Aupora's body and the change in her expressions informed Aniket that she had got the message loud and clear but did not want to accept the words. 'Stop it Aniket! It's not funny! Enough of this crap!' Aparajita was both furious and embarrassed. After that she went quiet and sat away from him.

'Aupora don't look so upset. I am not joking. Even that day I was not. But I did not have the courage to see you so upset. Yet I have to tell you. I can't go on like this,' Aniket pleaded.

'You don't have to say anything right now,' he said after a while. 'Try and understand, think it over. You are all that I really want in my life. I have loved you for so long and can't live without you.' Aniket implored again and tried to break through to her with his sincere justifications. But she stood like a statue, neither moving nor responding in anyway. 'I had to tell you this. I want you to be my girlfriend. Will you?' Aniket asked, looking a little silly and funny at the way he suddenly bent down and stretched out his hands. But Aupora did not respond. He stood up after a while and became silent, waiting for Aparajita to open up. None spoke. Both just kept standing, each lost in their own thoughts.

Aupora's thoughts were in disarray. She was indeed dumbstruck. *What was happening? Was Aniket joking again? But why would he look so serious then and stretch it so far as to make it embarrassing?* She felt dizzy and very confused. 'I…I need to leave,' was all she said. She left in a hurry leaving a very sad

Aniket rooted to the spot and looking at her receding figure longingly.

45

'Montu, you know what you have to do. Good luck now,' Ritesh told his friend as they dispersed at the entrance of the resort which was decked up from top to bottom with lights. *Tonight – It must be quite a huge event.* Ritesh thought to himself as he saw all the arrangements being made. Almost the complete area was decorated with flowers and lights.

'I am here to meet Mr Chabra,' Ritesh informed at the reception. 'Your name, sir?' asked a pretty receptionist. 'Ritesh,' he replied. 'I have an appointment with him for 7:30 pm,' he further informed her. 'Okay sir, please wait, I will just inform him.' 'Thank you,' Ritesh replied flirtatiously. *The girls here are 'good lookers'*, Ritesh thought as he found himself getting distracted by the extremely fair-looking, slim girl who was assisting him. 'He will join you in a while,' the girl informed him. 'Okay thank you,' Ritesh said for a second time. He was nervous and excited. Things are going as planned till now, he thought. They just had to ensure one last time, whether Chabra was as good as his word. And that he was ready to do business with them without any danger to them or their gang.

'Are you from the same town?' he tried to distract himself by chatting up with the lovely girl again. 'Yes I am,' the girl replied. She found the boy quite handsome. She was curious about him and wanted to know more. But the hotel rules forbade her to interact more than necessary with hotel guests.

In Pursuit of Ecstasy • **177**

Plus this one was here to see the 'big boss' himself. 'Listen when do you finish your shift?' Ritesh asked the girl. '…In a couple of hours…Why do you ask?' She knew the answer but just wanted to make sure.

'Oh well, I have come here for the first time and am quite keen to see the town. I was wondering if you could be my guide for the evening and show the place around to me,' Ritesh said charmingly. 'Well I don't know,' she said, but actually was thrilled at the idea. 'Don't worry…Rita,' Ritesh read her nameplate and cut into her thoughts '. . . I am a perfect gentleman. Just dinner and a good, evening stroll. Okay?' he asked turning on his fatal smile. 'Mmm…okay. Sounds good. Say around 9:30 pm then?' The girl agreed unable to resist him. 'Sure.' Just then a man walked up to him. 'You are here to meet Mr Chabra?' he asked looking grimly at him.

'Yes,' Ritesh replied undaunted by the man's unfriendliness. 'Okay. Please come with me. This way.' He went ahead. Ritesh winked at the girl and went after him.

Meanwhile Montu mingled with the crowd of employees who were busy carrying out orders for the evening event. He had worn an old pair of black trousers and a grey T-shirt to not attract much attention towards himself. His only give-away was his height and his large frame. But nothing much could be done about that. He had decided to keep himself away from well-lit areas and try and be ready to go to assist Ritesh, if really needed. And to do some more fact-finding while he waited for Ritesh to finish up.

'So what is this event all about?' he asked a housekeeping boy, who was being instructed by the supervisor. The boy was too irritated and busy, so he simply said, 'What else…the

Boss is in town. Whenever he is here we all have to work like donkeys, one party after another.' And then he started off the round of complaints. 'I have not had a proper sleep for the last three nights. Can you imagine?' Montu nodded sympathetically '...They fill their pockets well and proper, while all we do is work, work and work.'

'I can understand *bhai*,' Montu said finally as he handed him a cigarette to smoke. 'Thank you, which department are you in?' The boy took it gratefully and asked Montu. 'Oh, I will join room service. Very new here,' Montu lied easily. 'Okay, okay, get ready to work your butt out.' The boy smiled at him. 'We can always do with extra hands. I believe room service is even worse.' The boy said taking in a strong puff. 'Oh is that so?' Montu pretended to be crestfallen.

'Yes especially now. These events we have around this time of the year...some cover the nearby forest area too. And that is tough to service. Besides they want the best.' 'What do you mean?' Montu enquired. 'I mean we have organised parties in the midst of the forest. I have heard they are lavishly thrown parties where you have a free supply of *nashe wala sutta, daroo aur ladkiyaan* (Drug laced cigarettes, alcohol and girls)...You know...' he informed in a hushed-up voice. '...The housekeeping staff keeps talking of these parties. Mind you, only a few of the most trusted staff is allowed in there. But the stories travel you know.' He winked and informed Montu, who was listening to every word intently. 'Hmmm...looks like I should quickly make myself a trusted staff then.' He laughed when the boy finished and the boy joined in on getting the joke. 'I swear, if I had done room-service training, I would have been definitely selected. I am quite loyal and good in my work.' He boasted about himself. Then hearing his name being called he quickly stubbed the half-burnt cigarette with his feet, said a quick – 'Be seeing you around' and left.

'Hello Ritesh, welcome welcome,' said the familiar voice. The short, pot-bellied man with neatly combed hair and a typical smell that reminded Ritesh of pure *desi ghee* greeted him cheerfully. Ritesh noticed that Mr Chabra had not changed a bit and neither the men responsible for his safety.

He quickly took in the scene as he smiled and greeted Chabra. 'How are you Mr Chabra? After long time we meet again,' he said as he shook his hands a little nervously. This man was one of the most ordinary looking yet the most dangerous of the peddlers Ritesh had known of or met. His power came from the fact that he had a very strong network and he was an old hand in this business. Though the police had been after him for the past several years, he had never got caught. Even Mamu was happy and would have continued doing business with him had they not feared about the police reaching them through Chabra and put their own business and lives in trouble. Mamu had been upset at the decision then, but the Lord's decision was always carried out. No one dared to question or refute it. That is why this time they needed to be completely sure that doing business with Chabra again will not put them in any kind of trouble.

'So Ritesh, how can I help you this time?' Chabra asked smiling superficially.

'Oh, firstly thank you for seeing me.'

'Hmmm...no problem. You are our old associate and we have done some good business, haven't we?'

'Yes yes...sure we have,' Ritesh agreed wholeheartedly. 'Well you see we have a really huge quantity this time. I cannot tell you the exact amount, but it is huge. Much bigger than any of the deals we did last time.'

'Okay I get it. But tell me something Ritesh, why do you want to deal with me again? I mean you had pulled out suddenly when we were doing good business, right? So why do you want to come back now?' Chabra asked without much ado. Ritesh knew this would be one of his first questions. He was ready with the answer. 'Sir-ji, last time our boss was not so confident about your power and your reach and so was a little apprehensive in doing business with you. But he now knows from the market that in the North there is only one king – Mr K. Chabra,' Ritesh pumped him.

'Hmmm...okay...okay, good he knows that. But why should I resume my dealings with you?' Ritesh was again prepared. 'Three reasons sir. One, we have "stuff" of the purest quality. We can even show you a sample. Two, we have a fairly large quantity, so you need not go to ten different places to procure the stuff. And three, you would be making a huge profit. You are already rich, but you know how it is in this business, no harm if you get a good deal.'

'Okay. That sounds satisfying,' Chabra said after a while. 'But tell me why have you and your friend been snooping around my property?' Chabra asked a little sharply. For this Ritesh was unprepared. So he fumbled despite himself. 'We...oh we...were just...you know curious to see your place. Nice place you have here,' Ritesh replied unconvincingly.

'Come on Ritesh, let's not play cat and mouse games here. Tell me the real reason. You practically did a thorough research on me and my property. Spoke to some of my old staff members here. Did a recce of the place. Took the resort's events list. I know everything.' Chabra smiled his 'Don't play with me coz I know it all' smile. Ritesh knew he was in trouble well and proper.

'Okay, I will tell you,' Ritesh said accepting defeat. 'Mr Chabra the deal we want to make with you is worth over twelve crores and you in turn will earn even more. So you can imagine what we are talking about here.' Ritesh paused for the effect. But Chabra remained silent and elusive. 'We need to be absolutely sure that you will not only deliver but that the whole transaction will be carried out safely. We just needed to find out on our own. So we did what we had to. We had to be confident to convince our big boss about this partnership.'

'And what have you found out my friend?' Chabra asked keeping his thoughts to himself. 'Well, to tell you honestly we have reached the conclusion that you are much better off and secure than we had hoped you would be.'

'Hmmm…thank you my dear friend. I am happy that you opened up and were honest. If you had lied even a bit, you don't want to hear what would have happened to you and your dear friend who I know is waiting for you somewhere inside the resort area.' Chabra was saying all this smiling but Ritesh knew that what he had said was not only a threat but also the truth. He shuddered at the thought of what would have happened had he lied.

'Well Mr Ritesh, I am keen to do this transaction with you, provided I check the sample myself and find it half as good as you proclaim it to be. I will also procure 'OK' reports about you people,' Chabra laid down his conditions. Ritesh raised an eyebrow and had begun to say something, but Chabra impatiently cut him off. 'You see we also must know about your state of health before we do business with you again. Don't you agree?' he asked as if he was being most reasonable. And Ritesh knew he was.

Ritesh looked at him glumly and nodded. 'Yes of course!' he mumbled thinking Mamu might not be too pleased with this news. 'Mr Chabra I have to go back to report to my boss about all this. Then if they agree, you can also visit us or send your man down to Kolkata and then we can take care of things from thereon.'

'Yes. Fair enough. My man will come but you won't know about it. If he is satisfied he will contact you to collect the sample. Once your Mamu…isn't that the man we dealt with last time?' Chabra enquired. Ritesh nodded and marvelled at Chabra's memory. 'Okay so when Mamu agrees to it and once we are okay with it, things will move ahead,' Chabra finished.

Ritesh, curious about something, asked Chabra who now looked impatient. 'Just a last question – Incase things work out, where will we deliver this? And can we expect full payment upon delivery?' 'Well…our man who will contact you will let you know. I will brief him. And now I really have to go,' he said urgently. '…There are people waiting for me. So thank you once again. Enjoy the rest of your stay in Shimla and hopefully we will meet again.' Chabra finished and got up. This forced Ritesh to leave his seat too. He shook the outstretched hands and left feeling the same way as he had entered – excited and nervous!

'So how did it go?' Montu asked his friend as soon as they met at the badly-lit corner, just outside the resort. 'Well, let's get out of here first,' Ritesh hissed hurriedly as he walked past Montu in the dark and gestured him also to keep walking.

Ritesh relaxed once he reached the hotel. He was sure Chabra's men must have kept a watch on them till they had left the resort completely. He had so looked forward to meeting the recently befriended receptionist after his meeting. But he had left her gaping at his back as he made a quick exit.

'Ooh...that was some thing,' Ritesh said looking relieved as he collapsed into the chair in his room. He had not been very sure whether Chabra's men would have left the two alone without confronting them. But to his utter relief they had.

'The thing is...we thought we were being smart. But they were one up on us. They knew everything,' Ritesh informed Montu who looked equally shocked. 'Anyways the good news is Chabra is keen to do business with us again. Though he is sceptical and will do his own research.' Ritesh narrated the details of the meeting to Montu.

'Hmm...so we have to make sure that Mamu agrees to his conditions. Sample checking is no problem. But his men coming and snooping around. Mamu might not like it. What is the guarantee that they will buy from us?' Montu asked the question that had been playing in Ritesh's mind. 'And what if they come to know that we are desperate to sell? Will they not try and bargain?'

'Hmmm...I know, but we don't have options. We have to be on our guard the whole time. No talking to strangers from now on. Tell all the boys. No talking means no talking. Okay?' Ritesh ordered Montu who like always nodded in total agreement.

46

'What's wrong Aupora? Tell me please? Why do you look so dazed and puzzled?' Deep asked her friend for the hundredth time. Though she had an idea of what must have happened and her own heart was racing. But she was more concerned about Aparajita right now.

'Come on tell me? What is it? Someone hurt you?' she asked again. 'No Deep much worse.' Aupora then looked at Deepanita and said, 'Aniket...Aniket...he says he loves me. Finally Aparajita broke her silence. 'At first I thought he was joking or something. But he was not. He was serious. How could he? I mean, I never thought of him in that way. He is a good friend...' She trailed off as she felt very confused.

Was it true? Did she really think of him as just a good friend? Did she not always depend on him for every small thing before he had annoyed her by divulging things to Siddharth? Did she not like the fact that he had no girlfriends, even though there were plenty ready to fall all over him? Did she not enjoy all the pampering and attention he showered on her? She was more puzzled than ever before.

'I think I need to sleep,' Aparajita told a tired Deepanita who had also given up on her friend for now. 'We will talk tomorrow Deep. Let's just sleep over it tonight.' 'Do you need anything?' she asked Deepanita. 'No thanks,' responded her friend worried and preoccupied with questions of her own which didn't seem to have any answers. 'Okay. Goodnight then.' Aupora gave a wry smile to her and switched off the bed lights.

The trip back to Kolkata was as chaotic and noisy as it had been on their way to the hillstation. The last day was spent buying souvenirs from the mall for all those back in Kolkata. But Deepanita who had recovered sufficiently to walk on her own noticed that both Aparajita and Aniket had become strangers to everything and everyone.

Aparajita had still not opened up about her feelings for Aniket. And try as she did Deepanita could not bring her to respond in her usual way. In fact she hardly spoke to Aniket who was himself trying very hard to win her again. Aparajita went to greater lengths to avoid him. She knew she was breaking her promise to him. But she needed this space between them. She was seeing him in a new light. And she wanted to be sure of her feelings before she gave him any answer.

Aniket on his part had become sad and reclusive too and to Deepanita's horror, he was now openly getting drunk every other day. She was more concerned for him than for Aparajita.

'Aniket, please. Do you think you should drink so much?' she confronted him the night before they were leaving for Delhi. 'Oh leave me Deep. I know what I am doing,' he told her rudely, snatching the beer bottle back from her hands. 'I am a goo…d b…u…oy, you seeee! A very…good boy. My mother taught me to be one like my fa…ther. But good boys…good boys…don't get good girls! So what is the use of becoming a good boy? Let m…e be a bad buuuuoy now,' he said smiling silly and slurring on his words. Deepanita felt like hugging him. But she knew she dare not let her own feelings get involved in this and make it even messier. But she was pained. She now became sure that both her friends did love each other but were unable to see it as of now. She also knew she had lost Aniket.

He loved Aparajita deeply and would never see her in the same light. Her pain was as much for her friends as it was for her own self too.

BACK IN KOLKATA

47

'So how was the trip?' Sushanto asked Ritesh in the evening when he came back from college. Sushanto had been busy preparing for the dance competition. But many of his students had also gone for the trip so he had not prepared the sequences of the dance drama yet. There was a lot to be done. And he wanted his group to win the competition. That would teach all his critics a lesson.

He had spent countless nights thinking about Ritesh's dealings with Mamu. This problem was ten times bigger than the dance competition. Ritesh's and his own future depended on the success of this deal. *I hope things work out well for us.* He continuously prayed to his Shiva.

He gestured Ritesh to come and sit next to him on the sofa as he repeated his question. 'Coming Dada. Let me just freshen up,' Ritesh responded. 'Hurry up. I have to go out in a while.'

Ritesh joined him after changing into his home clothes with a Coke in his hand. 'Do you want one?' he asked his elder brother. 'No thanks. Tell me, what happened there?' Sushanto asked, impatient for the update.

'Well, the news can be good or bad. It depends on how Mamu and you take it.' 'Meaning?' Sushanto asked sharply.

'Dada, Chabra is keen to do business with us, provided his man comes down here, does his own "fact finding" about us and is confident that we can deliver. He also wants us to send him a sample first. The same man will collect it. And of course after that he will be ready to do business with us and does not mind paying the complete sum in cash.' Ritesh informed his brother who was listening intently.

'But Ritesh,' Sushanto began to protest at the laid-down conditions. 'Dada please let me finish,' Ritesh gestured his brother with his hands to listen to him first. '. . . Montu and I did a thorough check on the man. It seems that his network has become better and stronger than before. No doubt he is well connected and loaded. There is no way that the police can even get near to smelling "it" but even if they do, he can take good care of it. We just have to ensure that our travel from Kolkata to Delhi or wherever he wants us to deliver the "stuff" is "leak proof".' Ritesh finished with a triumphant smile.

'I have full faith in your capabilities. And you seem pretty confident about everything. So I guess everything is going to go well. But the worry is how to convey all this to Mamu. He will be furious to know that someone will be snooping around. And how can we be sure that the man will not double-cross us and go some place else for business? We have a lot to lose.'

'That is a risk we will have to take, Dada. Chabra does not look the type to get himself involved in such small things. Besides, he knows us, has worked with us in the past and has also found us to be profitable. Why would he take unnecessary risks? That too when the stuff is in huge quantities, not everyone has that kind of amount readily available. Even we can't risk keeping it for long,' Ritesh justified. 'Besides we too, will be alert. I will tell all my boys to be on their guard. In fact, Montu and I have already discussed that,' he said trying to ease his brother's worries.

'Hmm...you are right. Smart thinking!' Sushanto said after a while, allowing himself a small smile for the first time in days. *The plan was taking shape indeed. Now only Mamu should agree.* He thought to himself. 'Okay we will go tomorrow. Let me fix an appointment with him.' Sushanto made up his mind and informed his brother. He came up to Ritesh, ruffled his hair affectionately and went away to make the call. Ritesh felt much relieved. He felt happy that half the battle had been won.

48

'Aupora *beti*, why do you look so sad?' Kobita walked in with her milkshake and asked Aparajita who was lying on her bed looking gloomy.

'Uh...huh...nothing Pishi I am fine,' Aparajita lied, taking the milkshake from her caretaker and whom she always thought of as her second mother. 'Something is wrong. Aniket tries to call, you refuse them. You don't even speak to Deepanita properly. What is the matter child? Tell me? Someone bothering you?' Kobita asked her lovingly. '*Ki korbo Pishi?*' (What shall I do?). She broke down on hearing the loving voice. 'Arree...Areee...don't cry.' Kobita was alarmed. 'Tell me now? What happened?' she sat down on the bed feeling really concerned. Aparajita rarely broke down.

'Ani...ket...Aniket proposed to me,' she blurted out. '...But he is my friend. I don't think of him in any other way. Now if

I refuse him I will also lose a good friend. We can never have the kind of relationship we shared. Even if we stay friends, it will all be artificial and strained. And I am all so confused. I do not want to lose him. But I don't know whether I like him in that sense or not.'

'There...there *ma*...that is all,' Kobita smiled. She had known that this day would come sooner or later. And she liked Aniket. He was a good boy and very good for Aparajita. But Aparajita had to realise that herself.

'Aniket is a good boy. And your best friend. You cannot lose him. Why should you? Now *ma* you have to get married some day or the other. Here is your best friend, proposing to you. And you like him a lot, don't you?' she asked lovingly, to which Aparajita nodded. '...So why don't you give him a try? See whether you like him in that sense or not.' She paused and laughed as Aparajita blushed. 'And if you do, then go ahead. Isn't that better than sulking and crying cooped-up in your room?' the wise maid asked the girl. 'Hmmm...you are right!' Aparajita sat up on the bed. *The idea was more than good. Why did it not strike her before?* 'Pishi you are an angel.' She hugged her second mother lovingly.

Had she discussed all this with her own mother, she would have firstly given her a lecture and then might have asked her to stop seeing Aniket altogether. In fact Aniket was her favourite and she trusted him. But Babuji would have been furious, had he got even a wiff of it. He did not believe in the concept of 'Boyfriend & Girlfriend'. Now, Pishi had solved her problem so simply. Aparajita smiled to herself after many days. 'Okay now quickly finish your milkshake and get out of the room.' She found her Pishi ordering her.

'Hey Sid, wait up, where are you going?' Ritesh stopped Siddharth. He wanted to thank him for agreeing to help them out in Shimla. But he was glad that they didn't require him in the end. 'Mmmmm...oh just to the library.' Siddharth had seen a quiet Deepanita minus her friend walking towards the library. And since he was free too, he decided to follow her. But now Ritesh stood blocking his path. 'Well, I just wanted to thank you for being a good sport.' 'Yeah okay. But take care in future. And to tell you honestly, you should try and stay away from such dangerous things,' Siddharth tried to warn him, knowing deep inside that it won't cut through and may even rub the wrong way. 'Hahahaa...' Ritesh laughed amused, '...don't tell me that...and what's up with you? Turning into a good boy are we?' he said sarcastically. He hated to be lectured on morals and talks of good and evil. He was happy the way he was. And even though his elder brother wanted to keep him away from the business once he finished college, he had other plans.

Getting no response from Siddharth and finding him looking at a distant figure he said, 'I can see your interest in the pretty *chashmish* is deepening. I must check her out too,' Ritesh remarked giving a sly smile.

'Hey, stay away from her and don't talk about her like that,' Siddharth flared up. 'How cheap can you be? I warn you–stay away from her.' He said angrily and not satisfied yet, pushed Ritesh.

'Oh come on! Cool it buddy!' Ritesh didn't want to create a scene although he was totally pissed with the way Siddharth had responded to him. The reason was simple – Sushanto had asked him to keep a low profile. Besides, Siddharth had done him a favour earlier.

'Now take this from me, don't ever even think about Deepanita. Leave her alone.' Siddharth warned again before walking away disgusted and very upset. 'We are quits buddy. I will have my day too,' Ritesh said to his receding back and went the other way not caring whether Siddharth had heard him or not.

'Mamu, we can pull this off for sure. Think about it with a cool head,' Sushanto was trying hard to convince his uncle. He had come with Ritesh, to his uncle's house on the appointed date. Thereafter, Ritesh had narrated the whole story including his own findings and Chabra's final conditions to Mamu. Mamu had listened intently till the part where Ritesh mentioned 'the conditions'.

Those conditions got him excited and he did not want anything to do with the drug peddler from Delhi. 'How can I do that?' he said angrily. 'Someone will come from outside and check us out? How dare he even suggest that?' Mamu said excitedly. Sushanto intervened to appeal to his uncle's better sense. 'Let him come. He will find us as healthy and strong as anyone or even better. After all we are old and strong in this business and have a name too. We need not be scared.'

'Scared? Who says I am scared?' Mamu got even wilder. 'I don't like anyone snooping around my property,' he clarified angrily. 'Okay Mamu sorry. Yes I understand. But we did snoop around about him too, right? And besides we need this guy right now,' Sushanto stressed. '…The Lord will not give us extra time. He wants his balance sheet well and proper when he visits us in December or January.' Sushanto tried out his trump card. It worked. The Lord's name calmed Mamu down for the moment.

'Okay I will do it,' he said after much contemplation. '…But Sushanto, you will be responsible for this whole project. Once this Chabra fellow has satisfied himself, and satisfied bloody well, he will be…,' Mamu smirked and went on '…and be ready to do business. You have to personally oversee every aspect. I will not have *kal ka chokras* mess up my business for any silly act of theirs.' He pointedly looked at Ritesh who meekly looked down, though inside he was seething with anger. After all he had not only devised a good plan, he had even carried out the execution part accurately, except one 'little' mistake – it had never occurred to him that Chabra's men had been keeping a tab on him and Montu.

'Mukherjee Saheb, you must understand, our Aupora *beti* is very talented. She has been picked up amongst so many others. Moreover, she is competing at a national level. Only four groups have been selected and Nritya is one of them. I did some fact-finding and came to know that the the group is prestigious and famous and has a strong chance of winning this competition. They will bring accolades to our state. Won't you like Aparajita to be a part of that? Even Aniket is going for it.' Mr Joydeep Choudhary was making his case stronger and stronger. But Aparajita's father's face was a blank mask. He just kept listening to Mr Choudhary. Finally when Mr Choudhary had finished defending his client, he waited for the result of his case. 'Joydeep, I will consider it. I really don't like Aparajita to waste her time here and there. But as you said, this is a national event and there is a possibility of the group winning and brining honour to our state. I will give it a serious thought. But let me also speak to Aupora first. Okay?' he smiled, firmly putting an end to any further argument or discussion on it.

Aniket who had been sitting quietly beside his father knew nothing further could be said or done on the matter, so he excused himself and went out towards the kitchen. It was Aniket who had reminded and coaxed his father to not delay the matter anymore. And both had come visiting Mr Mukherjee after fixing an appointment with the busy minister. Aniket knew he had to somehow make Aparajita's father agree to let her go. Not only because he had promised Aparajita, but also because it would make her very happy. And he wanted to cheer her up. She had lately started avoiding him completely. Awkwardness had creeped into their relationship. She was also always careful to avoid any conversation about their Shimla trip. He was thus desperate to win her back again. And this was a brilliant opportunity.

'Pishi Aupora *kothai*?' (Where is Aparajita?) Aniket asked Kobita. She looked at the boy who really looked as if he could do with some cheering up, smiled at him gently and replied. 'As usual in her room. Go…go to her. She will feel good. She has been feeling rather low. . .' and left her sentence hanging midway. Aniket thought about it for a while and then said, 'Yeah okay, I think I will just say hello to her.'

Aparajita heard rather than saw Aniket first. She had trained herself to identify the different approaching noises as a precaution. Though her parents rarely visited her, yet she did not believe in being careless.

'Hi Aupora,' Aniket had a nervous smile on his face as he stood at her doorway looking uncertain.

'Oh hi! Come in. Why are you standing there?' Aparajita found herself feeling quite shy and awkward. These feelings were new to her and made her tongue-tied whenever she met Aniket nowadays.

'Actually Babuji wanted to see your father. So I came along,' he said casually not wanting to disclose the purpose of the visit straight away.

'Oh okay,' Aparajita replied.

'Aupora, I have to say something to you,' Aniket took a chance, seeing Aparajita looking relaxed. 'Yes?' she suddenly was on guard again. 'Aupora, see what I said that day in Shimla, it does not change anything between us. We are still good friends and will always remain so. Please don't behave so strangely and look so worried when I am in front of you,' Aniket implored. Aparajita looked at her friend. He really was sincerely trying to make up with her. She was the one who had been avoiding him. And as Kobita Pishi had shown her – *Unnecessarily!!!*

Making up her mind she smiled and said, '...Okay Aniket, you are right. I am also tired of playing hide-and-seek with you, ' she paused and noticed Aniket smiling at her choice of words.

'Let us give our relationship a try. Okay?' she asked him looking shy and naughty. Aniket jumped up in excitement, 'Really? Aupora...Really?? Am I hearing it right??? I love you and will always keep you happy...you mean so much to me.'

'Hey calm down.' Aparajita laughed at the boyish excitement of her 'best friend turned boyfriend'. Aniket grabbed her and hugged her tightly. She was still laughing. 'Okay okay, enough.

Get away and don't shout, you will bring the whole house down.' She ended with a shy laugh. Aniket wanted to kiss her. But just then they heard someone approaching. 'Pishi,' Aparajita said quietly to Aniket's raised brows. 'Aupora, Baba *daak che,*' (Your father is calling you) Kobita informed the smiling teenager. The smile vanished. 'Why?' she asked Kobita. 'I don't know. Come down and find out,' Pishi replied enigmatically. Both Aniket and Aparajita followed her downstairs.

'Aupora *kaimon achho*?' enquired Mr Choudhary jovially, as soon as he saw her walk into the room with Aniket. 'I am good Uncle, thank you,' Aparajita answered and bent down to touch his feet. He blessed her lovingly.

'Aupora,' she heard her father call her. 'Why did you not tell me about you being selected for this national dance competition?' her father asked her gravely. 'Baba, I was going to,' Aparajita replied alarmed and looked away from his eyes confused at what was happening. Then she suddenly remembered, *Mr Choudhary was here – on the mission.*

She glanced at Aniket and started, 'Errrr, Baba actually I refused. Uh…huh…Aniket insisted me to at least appear for the auditions. I complied. And…and got selected also Baba'. She tried to put some cheer into her voice. His father heard her explanation and looked at Aniket, who stood silently, looking foolishly at Aparajita first and then back at her father.

'Hmmm, Aupora, you should have told me this before, I am proud of you. Joydeep told me you and Aniket got selected out of hundreds of others. Is it true??' he asked looking at Aparajita, who looked non-plussed. 'Yes, yes uncle very true,' Aniket said. 'Hmmm, I am happy for both of you. Go for it and get the trophy home. Okay??' He praised his daughter. 'Baba,' Aparajita laughed and cried at the same time and gave her dad a warm hug. 'Thank you so much Baba. I am so happy. And of course we shall win!' she said between her tears and smile. 'Okay okay, go now. We have some other discussions to do,' her father affectionately patted her and responded.

49

Both the teenagers came out of the room, smiling from ear to ear. 'Aniket, thank you so much,' Aparajita held his hands tightly and said as soon as they were out of earshot. 'You are more than welcome Aparajita. I knew this would make you happy. And I want to see you smile always,' Aniket remarked smiling. He too was happy. It was then that Aparajita realised that how deeply Aniket loved her. The knowledge thrilled and gladdened her heart.

'Deep, Deep, Aniket and I we…are…errr…going around. I mean we are a couple now,' Aparajita informed her best friend as soon as Aniket left with his dad. 'I accepted his proposal,' she gushed on; unaware of the fact that gloom had descended at the other end of the phone. 'Deep, are you there?' she asked after a while, on getting nothing except silence from the other end of the phone.

'Oh…yes…yes…I am very much here. It is wonderful news…I am very happy for you two,' Deepanita replied faking her cheer. 'Oh for a moment I thought you had kept down the phone or something,' Aparajita replied a little puzzled at her friend's insipid response.

'Listen I need to go. Ma needs me. We will talk later.' She quickly kept down the phone before the tears that had formed a lump in her throat threatened to give away her 'long kept' secret. This was one of the saddest days of her life. She had loved Aniket and had even thought that things would be all right once he realised that Aparajita did not love him. But things never did work out the way she wanted. For the rest of the day she did not venture out of her room and the next few days missed her college on the pretext she was feeling unwell. There was no charm left for her to go there. It would instead remind her of the pain she had inflicted on herself.

'Dada! Dada! Chabra called today!' Ritesh walked into the house sounding all excited. 'Hey calm down, calm down, you are crashing in like a...like a crazy bull let loose. And keep your excitement and voice low,' Sushanto half scolded his brother gently. 'Sit down first, and then tell me what happened,' he ordered feeling equally excited but trying to control his emotions.

'Oh Dada I am so happy today, ' Ritesh unable to control his excitement, went on, jumping in a clownish manner before finally deciding to sit next to his brother who was smiling at his brother's little performance. 'Dada, his man was here,' Ritesh said, referring to Chabra. 'And I guess, he was quite happy with whatever he found out about us. They are ready to do business with us. Isn't it good news Dada?' Ritesh looked school-boyishly happy and excited. His brother smiled and nodded, 'Yes, indeed it is.'

'Okay. So one hurdle crossed. Now we have to work on our next step. How to carry so much of *maal* – they want it to be delivered to Delhi, without any risk,' Ritesh mused getting sober. 'Well for that I had another plan in mind and now we can club the two. No one will suspect anything about it,' Sushanto disclosed.

'What? You never told me?' Ritesh looked incredulously at this disclosure and felt hurt. 'Not everything can be disclosed even to you Ritesh. I had to keep a back-up plan ready just incase the Chabra guy refused. And anyways nobody knows about it. So don't look so disheartened,' Sushanto tried to comfort his younger sibling.

50

'Anyways, the plan is like this. My dance troupe is going for this competition to Delhi in December. I had planned and still plan to carry most of the stuff with us. Each member can carry at least 50 g, without raising any undue suspicion. I was however worried about how was I going to dispose off such a huge quantity and was thus preparing a list of all the possible people who could help me and whom I needed to contact before our trip,' Sushanto looked up to see whether his brother was listening intently.

'...But this is quite a dangerous plan. Since we might have had to deal with several people and there is a big chance that some might not be true to their word. But this was the only possible back-up plan I could think of at that time,' Sushanto said gravely.

'...But now since Chabra and Mamu both have agreed, we won't have problems. We can deliver the goods directly to him in his pub. In fact we can organise a dance party at his club and ask him to invite all his clients to it. It will be a win-win situation for both of us. In fact, our own boys and girls can also join the party and that way no one will suspect anything amiss at all. It will be a regular teen party – a very good camouflage to justify our presence as well,' Sushanto ended looking very pleased.

'Bravo Dada. Bravo. You are too good,' Ritesh said getting excited again. The plan was indeed faultless, he thought admiring his brother for it.

'Now we just need to let Mamu know of this execution plan. And we can get ready for it,' Sushanto said with a gleam of satisfaction in his eyes.

'Deep why are you not coming to college? It has been so many days now. You don't even answer my phone. Aunty told me you were not well. What happened? What is it?' Aparajita asked looking at her friend who looked all right to her except a bit pulled down and very sad. 'Oh, nothing much, just some lower abdomen pain. Bacterial infection, the doctor said,' Deepanita lied. She had even lied to her parents and brothers who were equally worried for her. 'I am on antibiotics, so taking rest.' She had bought some antibiotics from her regular chemist and had kept it in her room to fool the others.

'Oh Deep…Are you sure?? It has been so many days. You should be feeling better now,' Aparajita enquired not so sure of her friend's explanation. 'Yes, much better. I will start coming from tomorrow,' replied Deepanita who did not want her friend to suspect anything amiss. 'By the way, congratulations to you. Aniket and you really look good together.' Deepanita attempted a smile. 'Thanks Deep.' Aparajita smiled shyly. 'He is really so sweet. I wonder why I did not realise all this earlier,' she gushed. 'Hmmm...he is,' Deepanita nodded sadly.

'Hey look guys, the *Chashmish* arrives minus her bodyguard. Where is your bodyguard *haan*? Oh sorry, your best friend or your mother?' Ritesh teased Deepanita as she crossed them in the long corridors that led to her classroom. No response. 'Anyways, whatever. Can't see her around,' Ritesh mocked again when they had spotted Deepanita walking all alone towards her classroom. And Ritesh remembering how Siddharth had misbehaved with him for this girl thought of troubling Deepanita to take his revenge. 'Move from my way,' Deepanita said glaring at the boys. None budged. 'Oh ho, she is not scared of us. Is she?' Ritesh asked his friends in mock surprise. '*Miss Chashmish*,' he started moving close to her and would have gone on had not a strong hand from his back yanked him away from her.

Surprised and irritated Ritesh looked back saying, 'What the f...?' But he stopped mid sentence when his eyes recognised the figure. Siddharth glared at him angrily. 'I told you to stay away from her. You didn't listen then, but now you will,' saying that he boxed Ritesh hard on the face. The blow fell on his lips which became swollen and had started bleeding. 'No, Siddharth please...leave him,' alarmed at the sudden turn of events Deepanita implored to his better sense.

The approaching footsteps and the authoritative voice of the principal who was on a round dispersed the small group hurriedly. 'You will pay for this Siddharth,' Ritesh hissed before moving away.

'Are you okay?' Siddharth asked a shaken Deepanita. 'I am fine. But you should not have done that. They are very rowdy boys,' Deepanita said worriedly. 'Oh don't worry I can handle them,' Siddharth allowed himself a small smile to ease her fears. Deepanita smiled back shyly. 'Thank you for helping me'. Siddharth kept looking at her without saying or acknowledging anything. She felt her heart-beat quicken. 'Oh, I must go…have a class,'she said and excused herself. 'Bye Deep. Take care. And don't worry, those guys won't trouble you anymore,' Siddharth called after her back. She looked back and nodded in understanding and gave him her trademark smile. But somehow it seemed a little sad this time. He stood there watching her well after she was out of his view wondering why did she look so melancholic today? Maybe she was too frightened. He answered his own question. *Oh how I love to see her smile. I wish I see it every day of my life.* He smiled to himself at the chain of his now very familiar thoughts. *I love you Deep. How can I tell you I am so totally in love with you?* He confessed to himself. Then his face was grave again. *I must keep a watch on Ritesh and his gang. They will try to harm her again. I can never let that happen again.* He promised himself.

'Montu the plan has been approved by Mamu. We will be carrying the stuff along with Sushanto Da's dance troupe to Delhi. Call the boys. We need to select a few to accompany us in December for that trip.' 'You mean we are also going?' Montu asked a bit surprised. This was the first time they would be doing any such thing.

'Yes of course stupid. We have to go,' Ritesh said nursing his wounded lips. 'And we must teach that girl and her friends a lesson. They are a part of Sushanto Da's group. I saw the list yesterday,' he said smiling cruelly.

'*Saala* Siddharth! He hit me so bad just for that petty girl. I will teach him a lesson too. Thinks he is the boss of the college just coz he became the college captain,' Ritesh said angrily. '*We* were the reason he won and he forgot us so conveniently. Both will suffer for this.' Ritesh had made up his mind to avenge his insult.

Montu, who was standing silently besides his friend to ensure that no one was listening to their conversation, kept nodding, listening to his friend but not liking the idea at all. He knew Sushanto would not have approved of Ritesh's current designs. In fact Sushanto had separately asked Montu to keep Ritesh away from any troublemaking. Montu had promised to do as much as in his power to see to it that his friend never overstepped his line and come under the principal's radar.

Siddharth had followed Ritesh and Montu to warn them again to stay away from Deepanita, but the high and excited voices of Ritesh had made him stop in his tracks for some reason and he found himself eavesdropping on them again. He already knew they were onto some big and dangerous project. He had come to know of that in Shimla. But that it involved Sushanto, the dance teacher and his group, which surprisingly consisted of Deepanita, Aparajita and Aniket and moreover which was going for some dance competition to Delhi for which Ritesh and a few of his other gang members would also be going…all these facts rang alarm bells in Siddharth's mind. He froze on his track for a moment. His mind numbed with all the information, puzzling him more than helping him find answers. *Why would Ritesh and all want to go with the dance group? Sushanto was actually Ritesh's brother? How had this fact never been disclosed to him anytime during his almost three years of interaction with Ritesh?* The unanswered questions just kept going round and round in his mind. *Oh I will go crazy like this. I must sort out all the information one by one. I need some peace of mind for that.* Deciding that, he stealthily walked back the same way he came and headed for the college canteen.

Sushanto was also involved in drug peddling? And that means he uses the dance group just as a camouflage! And they are working on some really big project. Maybe that involves carrying the drugs which Ritesh was mentioning as 'the stuff', from Kolkata to Delhi!!! And all the participants might be unknowingly involved in this illegal and highly dangerous activity including Deep. Siddharth did not know what to do when he reached the conclusion. *Oh god what will happen? How can I prevent all this? I can't even disclose anything to anyone. No one will believe me…I have no proof. How can I protect Deepanita?*

After racking his brains for a long while, he said, 'I will have to make amends with Ritesh and go with them on this trip and catch them red-handed.' He finally made up his mind.

'Okay girls and boys, we do not have much time. We have to practise really hard from now on – No letharginess or bunking of classes if you all really want to get the trophy home.' Sushanto informed the group, which was more than ready to give its best. They all wanted to win. This was a prestigious event and the possibility of Nritya winning the competition was really high. With these positive thoughts in their minds, the whole group shouted loudly and said – 'We will win, sir. We will win and get the trophy to our city.'

'Hmmm, that is like my team. We surely will win.' Sushanto had an enigmatic smile on his lips and a gleam in his eyes. His expressions confirmed one thing – he was superbly confident that they would win.

51

The weeks passed by quickly. Aparajita and Aniket came much closer to each other during this period. Aprajita found herself falling deeply in love with her best friend. She discovered many new things about Aniket. Most of all she felt herself blessed for having a partner who blended so perfectly with her and loved her unconditionally.

The only habit she found disturbing in him was his drinking. She noticed he had more than a passing interest in 'the bottle'. And slowly yet firmly she started keeping a tab on him and if he looked for any excuses to say — let's celebrate this — she would make sure it did not involve boozing. Of course she knew she could not be too strict with him. She believed, every man (and for that matter woman) deserved a bit of pint once in a while, as long as it did not control the man or woman. Aniket on his part was on top of the world. He could not have asked for anything more. He had got what he wanted. And he was ready to do anything for her happiness. Deepanita maintained a distance from them to give them more time together and to nurse her own wounds. However, she found Siddharth to be around her during this phase. For a while, she even suspected him of keeping a tab on Aparajita and her activities. He was always there, though mostly at a distance *Maybe we just bump into each other. It seems like he really has forgotton and forgiven Aparajita.* Siddharth would always acknowledge her and say hello. Nothing more.

'Okay class, we all leave day after tomorrow. No more practices. I have something to say to you all. Please take your seats,' Sushanto ordered his students after their final dress rehearsal was over. To his own satisfaction and to the delight and encouragement of the students it had been performed with perfection.

'Okay, firstly congratulations! You all have done well. Keep it up and we will surely win.' This was greeted with a cheerful applause from the the students.

'Now, we are taking a few souvenirs from here for the judges and organisers. As all of you know that there is a lot of luggage that needs to be carried for the dance performance including your heavy props, dresses, instruments and all, I want the packages and luggage items to be distributed amongst the complete group. I want each one of you to carry a package or a luggage item. The packages will not be too big. They will be well packed and you can put it inside your own suitcases or bags. The important point, I want to make here is, that many of the items are rare and very expensive. So I want each one of you to take special care of the items I give you. Are you all with me on this?' he asked. 'Yes Sir,' came the resounding answer from the students, few knew what they were actually getting into.

'Okay now, since this is a big event in which the college students from Presidency are also participating, we are assigning four students to look after the requirements of the students.

Their names are:
Siddharth Banerjee
Ritesh Mishra
Montu Ganguly
Divesh Das

They are all waiting outside. Let me call them in and introduce them to you.' As he announced the names, Deepanita and Aparajita exchanged glances. The names called out were of the college captain, Siddharth accompanied by his other office bearers who spelt trouble more than help. Deepanita was highly worried. But one look at Siddharth confirmed that he would take care of everything. Somehow that look made her feel comfortable and less worried.

'Deep, are you done for the day?' Siddharth asked, coming up to Deepanita who was standing and chatting with another girl from the same group. 'Oh...um...yeah I am. Tell me?' 'Okay, can you meet me at the café outside the college after ten minutes or so?' Siddharth asked her urgently, looking a bit worried.

'Yes okay,' Deepanita answered. She had of late found him to be pleasant and in fact more helpful towards, at least, her. She wanted to know what it was that made him look so worried and concerned.

'Okay Deep, whatever I tell you please keep to yourself,' Siddharth said after they settled down with their coffees. 'Don't ask me questions. Just understand one thing, this dance competition that you and the others are going for is a well-planned camouflage to carry out a dangerous deal. I can only tell you that you have to be alert the whole time and once you reach Delhi, give back the package to Sushanto as fast as you can. Tell Aparajita and Aniket also. Don't scare anyone. Just do it unassumingly,' Siddharth in his excitement just rushed through his words.

'What are you saying Siddharth?' Deepanita looked at him utterly clueless. 'See Deep you won't understand. And there is no need for you to understand it. You just need to keep the package safely and give it to Sushanto when you reach your destination. Just do your performance and come back. DO NOT...I repeat DO NOT try and get involved in any other activity of Sushanto's.' Siddharth said reflecting his contempt for the dance instructor. Deepanita caught this reaction and said, 'Why are you speaking of our sir like that? I am sorry, but I am not being able to understand any of this. Tell me clearly or don't talk about it at all? Are you trying to scare us away from the dance competition? Oh I get it you are trying to take revenge! You are cooking up a cock and bull story so that Aparajita and I miss the competiton and then later regret it.' Deepanita's voice was sharp. She was hurt. *How could he think like that? He hasn't changed and is still just the same.*

Siddharth gave up. He knew she would not trust him now. But maybe better sense will prevail later. He knew Deepanita to be a sensible person and now he was depending on it. 'Just remember my words. And you are free to go now,' Siddharth knew he could do no more. Deepanita left immediately, feeling puzzled and sad. She could not figure out why she was sad though.

'You know Aupora, yesterday Siddharth met me just after our dance class,' Deepanita informed her friend the next morning as she came over to her house. 'He did? He has the guts??' Aparajita asked angrily. 'Oh ho hold on. He never meant any harm. Listen. He told me something that is really puzzling,' Deepanita said cutting her friend in between. 'He said the packages sir mentioned to give us, has some suspicious...no he used the word dangerous stuff inside them. And we better be careful,' Deepanita disclosed.

'He also told me to take good care of them and as soon as we reach Delhi, we must hand it over to Sushanto sir and just concentrate on the dance performance. He was categorical that we should not indulge in any other outside activity which sir organises for us.'

'Hmm...sounds fishy,' Aparajita said after Deepanita finished, '...seems like he wants to play a big prank on us. Don't listen to him. You know how he is. Just forget about it. And concentrate on the packing.' Aparajita smiled at her friend, who smiled back but her heart somehow, was not relieved.

End of December 2008

DESTINATION DELHI

52

The train journey to Delhi was chaotic and fun. Each member of the group was over enthusiastic to help the other. But soon things settled down. Deepanita chose a seat a little away from Aparajita and Aniket. They protested but she insisted she preferred the particular seat next to the exit door than the one in the centre where Aniket and Aparajita were sitting. After a while the good humoured duo left her alone. 'Okay...come to our seat, once you settle in. You can go back when we bore you.' They suggested, looking lovingly at each other and then smiling at her. Deepanita smiled back. She had got used to them now. Though, it hurt her still to see Aniket so much in love with her friend. But she had adjusted herself to the situation.

Each member had received a package or a piece of luggage. Most of the girls got the packages and the boys the heavier luggage. Deep had still not been able to forget Siddharth's warning. From the little that she knew about Siddharth, she believed he was being genuine that day. *But why then...?* She was still very puzzled. 'Have you settled in nicely?' The voice that asked her this question, brought out an immediate sense of revulsion in Deepanita. Ritesh was smiling at her innocently as she turned around to look. 'I am fine thank you,' was all she said. She sat down on her seat and started reading Jane Austen's *Emma* that she had brought for the journey. 'Okay I can see you are quite busy,' Ritesh said in a teasing voice and got a nudge from Divesh to move on. *This boy gives me the creeps.* She thought to herself.

Late in the night, Deepanita wanting to go to the washroom got up, she had just walked a few steps when she overheard Montu telling Divesh, '...the stuff is real good. It will fetch us a very good profit. And all those who are a part of this project will become rich. I can finally hope to buy my car then.' Both laughed at something she could not catch as she crossed their curtained berths. Overhearing the two boys talking in this manner made Deepanita suspicious again and the warning that Siddharth had given her came rushing back to give her a sleepless night.

She had discussed the matter again with Aparajita a night before boarding the train. 'Forget it yaar. Siddharth was most probably lying,' Aparajita had said carelessly, too happy in the thought that she was after all going for the dance competition. 'But think Aupora, why would he lie? I mean he never pressurised me just cautioned me. And he looked damn serious,' she said ignoring her friend. '...He is himself going on this trip. Then he has saved me several times from that hooligan Ritesh. And btw (by the way) Siddharth's coming to this trip can still be understood, he is the college captain. But why are the two most notorious goons of the college coming on this trip? We did not even know that Ritesh was actually Sushanto sir's brother,' Deepanita would have gone on but Aparajita irritated and impatient had said, 'If there is any truth to what you are saying, we can hardly do anything about it now. Our parents won't understand anything. You know how difficult it was to get their permission, especially in my case.' She had paused over the phone for the necessary effect. Then after a while had gone on, '...Leave it *yaar*...let's just enjoy ourselves and do our best for the show. I am sure there is no truth to all this. Siddharth is either hallucinating or just wants to take revenge. He will not succeed though.' Aparajita had replied firmly ending the matter there.

Deepanita clamped up after that but continued to feel a strange restlessness which had increased after overhearing Montu's conversation. *I hope everything goes well.* She prayed to god silently.

Early morning they landed at Delhi. It was freezing cold. Siddharth had not slept most of the night. He had kept a watch on Ritesh and his gang. He suspected they might create some unpleasantness for Deepanita and her friends. Though he had mended his relationship with Ritesh, he found Ritesh to be no warmer towards him. And he also knew that if a good opportunity presented itself, Ritesh would play dirty with Deepanita and him. He did not want to give that opportunity to Ritesh.

I hope the inspector takes note of what I told him over the phone a few days back. I had given him enough evidence that I knew about this gang and the fact that they are about to peddle large amounts of drugs from Kolkata to Delhi. He seemed to believe me. I hope he follows us. Siddharth tried to ease his worry with the justifications. *A lot depends on that. The brothers and the whole gang can be caught red-handed, only thing is, the other students should not be there. I have to somehow ensure that the* maal *passes back to Sushanto before the dance event. Hopefully the inspector will listen to me and will come only during the event. God give me strength. I don't know why am I doing all this?* But his heart knew the answer. It was all for Deepanita. He wanted to see her safe and happy.

'Okay boys and girls, today we rest. Round one of the competition is going to be held tomorrow,' Sushanto was telling everyone. 'So check into your rooms and then we meet at the dining area for breakfast.' They were all booked in a guest house arranged by the organisers for them.

'Sir, what about the parcels?' Deepanita asked. 'Oh, take them with you and keep them safely. I will take them from each one of you separately.' This reply puzzled her. 'Why separately why not all together sir?' She was much relieved when another inquisitive girl asked him this question. 'Because my dear, we have to segregate the luggage and the packages according to how we need them.'

'We do not want things to go wrong towards the end,' Sushanto supplied a bit sharply. 'Okay sir,' replied the timid girl. Sushanto announced, 'Another thing before you all go, there is a dance party which has been jointly organised by us and a local admirer of our dance group. He is also a friend. He wanted to welcome the whole group. So he has invited all of us to his popular pub.'

'Yeahhhhhh!!!' cried everyone together. 'Okay okay...We will be leaving for that around 7:30 pm. So be ready accordingly,' Sushanto ordered and left.

53

Inspector Sukant Kumar had already boarded the train next to the one which carried the group Nritya to Delhi. A day before he boarded it, along with the rest of his special encounter team, the plan was chalked out to the last detail. The list of the complete group had been obtained from the college. A detailed background study of each and every student clearly showed that they all belonged to well-to-do families. In fact some of them were children of some prominent politicians and businessmen of the state. This was a big revelation and could give the police a big headache, if things turned bad.

The identity of the caller, who had given them the tip, however remained a mystery. It must be a person from the opposite gang or someone who has been wronged by Mamu or one of his gang members who had some grouse against the man. The inspector had cross-checked the information and had found it to be true. He reached the conclusion that there was a huge possibility that they could catch Sushanto and Ritesh red-handed. And they would lead him to Mamu also eventually.

Inspector Sukant had wisely called up some of the parents whom he knew could create a major problem for the police and had taken an urgent appointment with them to come and meet him. 'They are all involved sir. We do not know whether the children are knowingly or unknowingly a part of this. But we are planning a raid at their evening get-together at a local pub. I believe it will help us catch the culprit red-handed. We know that club. It is mostly frequented by youths from rich backgrounds. And rumours are that they organise 'rave parties' there,' Sukant continued to explain things patiently and politely. But the parents were agitated, angry and not ready to believe him at all. '...Sir I request you to please come to Delhi with me and witness the police raid for yourself. Maybe the children are innocent sir, but I have to do my duty. This is a grave matter.'

'Okay, we will come too,' replied a very angry Mr Mukherjee. He trusted his daughter completely. This was some kind of a trap. Maybe the opposition was trying to pull him down somehow...through his daughter. He made up his mind to go along with a few other parents including Deepanita's, Aniket's and Siddharth's who looked equally upset with the whole situation.

'Siddharth, you and Divesh will be the last to leave. Do ensure everything is locked properly. Okay!!' Sushanto ordered Siddharth. 'Rest of us will go first.' He had earlier asked the girls to carry their packets with them and give them back to him one by one (separately) for safekeeping. Aparajita and Deepanita were surprised that he was weighing each packet before keeping it but did not want to argue or ask questions. They just followed his instructions along with the other girls.

'Welcome, Nritya group...A very warm welcome to all of you,' Chabra was there with his men, Ritesh noticed. A big box was taken away from Montu's hands, which Deepanita suspected contained the parcels. The group was then ushered inside the pub. Inside, the party was already on. There were several youngsters on the floor. The DJ was playing some cool numbers. However, when the group arrived, the music stopped. Chabra introduced the group to everyone present and they were welcomed once again to Delhi. 'Enjoy yourselves but do not get too tipsy as the competition is starting from tomorrow,' Sushanto smiled at his group. 'Yes Sir!!!' some of the boys hollered, hardly meaning what they said. The girls just giggled in acceptance.

'Aupora, can I drink today?' Aniket asked, rather implored her. 'Mmmm...okay. But one condition,' she said naughtily. 'And what is that darling?' Aniket asked lovingly. 'I, too, will drink with you and then both of us will dance. Okay?' 'Oh yes, sure,' Anilket said laughing. 'I love you so much.' 'Me, too,' said Aparajita, '...I mean I love myself too.' She giggled walking towards the bar as Aniket followed her making a face.

Deepanita was feeling very uneasy. She had reason to be. Earlier her package had been slightly damaged by a nail which had been popping out of the table on which the parcel was kept. She had got an opportunity to take a quick peek inside it. And what she saw made her dizzy with worry and suspicion. It looked like 'white powder' packets. There was no way she could confirm anything and she could neither disclose it to anyone. For the first time in her life she was extremely frightened. Moreover, she had not been able to locate Siddharth.

As she stood worried in a corner, Ritesh came up to her with a glass of Mirinda. 'Okay, to our friendship. Forgive me for being rude earlier and troubling you,' he said smiling. She looked deep into his eyes. She knew he did not mean any of the words. But there was no escape. She took the glass from him and said a crisp 'Thank you'. He clicked his own glass with hers and said, 'Cheers!!' She was forced to mumble the same and drank some of it from her glass. Just then, Sushanto called out to Ritesh and he left her. She heaved a sigh of relief and drank some more. Soon she felt much relaxed and sat down in a corner. She noticed Aniket and Aparajita were dancing gaily, completely lost into each other, looking somewhat tipsy...so were few other couples from her group.

Suddenly Ritesh was by her side again. He had a plate with him in one hand and a glass of Mirinda in the other. He offered her the glass of the soft drink. By this time Deepanita was feeling light and happy, she took it from him. He sat down next to her and kept the plate besides him. It had the white powder packet she had noticed inside the parcel. He started playing with her hair. She felt scared now. Slowly his face came close to hers and kissed her lightly, removing her glasses. 'You are beautiful *chashmish*,' he said. She did not like his hands on her. But they were moving all over her body. She wanted to scream but all that came out was a small groan. This excited Ritesh more. 'Yes baby, I know you want it too,' he was saying. Frightened, feeling weak and paralysed she tried to raise her hands, but Ritesh caught them in his own and her attempt at screaming was drowned by the loud and blaring music The fear showed in her eyes as Ritesh's lips covered hers.

Siddharth walked in looking flustered. He had left Divesh behind, making some excuse. He knew Ritesh could try any of his dirty tricks on Deepanita. He might harm her. He swore under his breath for not making an effort to be with her earlier. He scanned the crowd. The lights were dim. And his eyes needed adjusting. But he was desperately commanding them to find her. When he did notice her finally it was already too late. Ritesh was bending towards a helpless Deepanita. Two things happened simultaneously, Siddharth ran towards them swearing and there was a loud bang. Everyone became still then. The music stopped.

'This is a police raid. Please do not move. The building is surrounded. Stay in your places.' Someone clicked him and the other youths who were now scared were trying to flee. Siddharth did not pay heed and moved towards Ritesh and Deepanita. But before he could reach them, an elderly gentleman reached her and slapped her hard on her face. She started crying.

EPILOGUE

February 2009

The judge was still reading his verdict, Siddharth realised as his mind jerked him back to the present. And suddenly anxious to know the collective fate of all his college mates including his own, he tried to concentrate and listen intently to to what the judge was saying. 'The Court imposes rigorous imprisonment of three months and a fine of ₹1 lakh on each of the convicts except Siddharth. They are first time offenders and have honestly accepted the fact that they travelled from Kolkata to Delhi with the knowledge that they were carrying something suspicious, given to them by the main culprits, but never reported it to the authorities despite getting a few chances to do the same,' the judge justified. 'Each so called parcel weighed about 60 g which is much more than the quantity legally allowed for personal possession.'

'...Further to that, all the offenders were also present at the party when the raid was conducted and had consumed small quantities of *'Ecstasy'*, all of which has been proved with prima facie evidence, medical examination and by witnesses (their own parents) present at the party. At the same time, the court also warns all the youths to take this as a fair warning and understand clearly that next time there will be no mercy for offences of such a serious nature.' The old judge paused for a brief while for his words to sink into the roomful of people. The crowd murmuring grew louder.

Resuming his judgment after a while the judge turned towards Siddharth, looked at him sternly before going on. 'Siddharth is however, sentenced to one complete year of rigorous imprisonment and a fine of ₹1 lakh for knowing everything yet keeping silent. This will be taken as abetting in the crime. Settling scores with college mates in this manner is dangerous for society at large. The court also hopes Siddharth Banerjee to understand this fact and learn something from this incidence.' Deepanita looked at him then. It was only she who knew the complete truth. He had no proof of proving his innocence. And she herself was an offender. Nobody would believe them. She kept silent.

April 2009

'Aparajita, Deepanita, you are being released today. Please freshen up and wear the pretty clothes sent by your parents yesterday. I am preparing your release orders. Do hurry up. And hey cheer up, your time in here is over. Think of the time you spent here as a serious punishment your college principal gave you, for doing something really naughty.'

The prison warden lady tried to buck up the young girls while handing them their freshly washed and ironed clothes and smiled kindly at both of them. She had grown fond of them in the small time they had stayed in the jail. Both silently looked at her and accepted the clothes. In the prison they had forgotten their 'trademark – Smile'.

As the girls came out of the prison they found Aniket, his parents and both their parents standing outside waiting for them. The girls still ashamed of letting themselves and their parents down so badly with their actions, walked slowly towards them with their heads bowed down. The parents however came forward and hugged them both warmly. It was then that Deepanita and Aparajita broke down. After the court hearing both had refused to talk or express any kind of emotion, even to each other. But on seeing their parents smiling so lovingly at them, neither could control themselves any longer.

'Deep, stop it darling. You have suffered enough,' said Deepanita's mother softly patting her daughter's head. 'We are really proud to have such a brave daughter, who accepted her mistakes openly. In fact, even we are to blame for what you did. Now, now, stop crying. Your brothers are waiting in the car. We all will go home and have a huge celebration for all of you. Isn't it?' Deepanita's mother looked at the other parents for encouragement who nodded back smiling through their own tears.

'Aupora, look up *beta*, there is no need to hide your face Aupora. Go to your Baba. See, he is also crying. Do you want to see him cry?' Aupora looked up then and noticed her father standing slightly away from the group. She went up to him and said incoherently through her tears, 'I…a..m re..ally sor..ry Baba. Plea..se fo..r..give me.'

'No *beta*,' her father said, '…it is I, who should say sorry. But you must promise me no more hide-and-seek games okay?' Aparajita smiled through her tears again. Aniket's mother came towards Aupora and hugged her. 'Your mom told me about you two. You both have my blessings.' The whole group laughed as Aparajita went scarlet and Aniket protested simultaneously.

December 2009

'Deep, hurry up! Our performance is next. I have prepared that speech we discussed.' Aparajita called out, looking extra tall and elegant in her dance costume which was peacock blue in colour and suited her complexion to perfection.

'What? And you are telling me now?' Deep said looking equally beautiful in her deep red costume. 'What if I fumble?' she said snatching the speech paper from her friend's hands and reading her lines.

'You won't darling. I have full faith in my best friend,' Aparajita replied laughing.

She and Deepanita had choreographed a dance performance which was going to be their last performance in their beloved college. It was a story-cum-dance enactment based on their recent experiences. This was their graduation day celebrations party. Usually graduation celebrations were organised separately for different streams. But this time round, the second and final year students of all the streams had decided to invite the complete college for the event and named it the 'Grand G - Day Party'. The planning and organisation of the event was done with much enthusiasm. Even the parents of the graduating students had been invited.

'It would have been wonderful if Siddharth were also here with us,' Aparajita said a little sadly while waiting for Deepanita to finish reading their speech note. On hearing his

In Pursuit of Ecstasy • **229**

name Deepanita's heart skipped a beat and she remembered the times in the previous year he had helped her. She had been puzzled by his kindness and gentleness towards her. And she had been equally perplexed by her own response to him. He had been an adversary then – Aparajita's and hers.

But strangely he did not behave so badly after her accident in Shimla. In fact after that he had become a good friend, who remained in the shadows and miraculously appeared only when she needed him. And she had almost fallen…Deepanita stopped her chain of thoughts. A good friend indeed, he had turned out to be. For some unknown reason she wished he was there to cheer Aparajita and her today and look at her with the same mesmerising gaze he had given her then. But of course he could not be there. There were still a few days left for his release and besides, there was no special reason for him to come to the college. He had already appeared for his final exams from the prison itself on a special request. The judge had listened to his parents' pleas and had allowed it. Aniket had informed her about all this.

'Okay let's go,' Aparajita pulled her out of her reverie. 'And all the best darling,' Aparajita said before moving out. Deepanita followed her with a thudding heart. As soon as their names were announced the whole college broke into rapturous clappings with cat calls and hootings following it.

As they came on stage, they requested for a couple of mikes. The audience slowly went quiet. Aparajita noticed Aniket holding his camera and blowing her a 'flying kiss'. She smiled back at him. She found her parents in the second row along with Aniket and Deepanita's parents.

'Dear Principal, faculty members, college mates, and our beloved parents, Deepanita and I have something to share with you all before we perform the dance choreographed by us,' Deepanita started.

'Many of you already know what we went through in the past year. It is not something one is proud of or would like to talk about but we decided to talk about it. And this is the best platform we can get. We want to set an example for many others like us. We want our stories to be told and known to each one of you so that it discourages you from doing what we did.' She paused for her words to sink in.

'The biggest mistake we committed, can any one of you tell us what it was?' Aparajita asked the audience. The crowd, started making noises and looked puzzled by this sudden turn of events. But no one answered or protested. Then suddenly a second year boy, who was known for playing pranks on teachers but never getting caught answered good humouredly, 'Well I think the mistake you guys did was that you got caught.'

The hall broke into splits of laughter. Aparajita and Deepanita stood silently till the noise died down. Then Aparajita replied, 'That was a smart answer but not the right one. My friend you are wrong. But it is not your fault, had I been in your place, even I would have thought and given the same answer,' saying this, Aparajita went quiet.

Deepanita took over '…The mistake we made was, in fact a mistake which is committed by most of us is, that we think of our parents as just a necessary machine, who are a constant in our lives. As those who provide for our education, entertainment and as people who are always nagging us saying, "don't do this, don't do that. Do this, be like your father, listen to your elders" and so on and so forth. Our adversaries! So consequently we start overlooking them or ignoring them. And that my dear friends, is the biggest mistake and the one, we also committed.'

'We did not want to share our feelings, problems, issues with our parents. We never believed that we should discuss, open up and communicate with them. We saw them as only hurdles in our lives. In fact, had I told my father of my suspicions, about the dance group, I guess things might have been different. But I just kept quiet, despite Siddharth having cautioned me about it. I refused to believe him and neither did I discuss it with any of the elders. Of course I did discuss it with Aparajita briefly but that was that. None of us felt it necessary to seek an elder's advice. We did not breathe a word about it to any of the parents. That was a huge mistake on our part. And I regret it to this day.' She paused for a while to control her emotions. Aparajita held her hands.

'...This past year or so has taught us how very important it is for us to open up with our parents. If we have to grow into a healthy and happy person we need to involve our parents in our lives. Thank you Mom and Dad! Thank you for your love and complete belief in us.' Deepanita looked at her parents and acknowledged them.

Then she continued, '... Of course, with due respect to all the parents and teachers present here, I must also admit that either parents are too busy to care for us or assume their role so seriously that they overlook the fact, that we are also individuals, each one of us different and with a unique personality and strength. You can impose on us to behave or do things against our basic nature but sooner or later we will either give up or just move away. You need to listen and listen very carefully to what we are trying to tell you instead of forcing your own views and ideas on us. Why make us clamp our feelings and lips in front of you when all we need is an understanding and loving attitude. That is all we wanted to say,' she ended her speech as suddenly as Aparajita had started it.

The audience remained silent, undecided and dazed. Deepanita was about to turn back to start the music, when her eyes caught a tall familiar figure, who started clapping first. It was Siddharth. He looked much leaner than before yet as handsome as before. Everyone else followed as if woken from a trance. The complete hall resonated with the sound of thunderous clappings and Deepanita found Aparajita smiling at both of their parents and Aniket who stood proudly with them clapping for both. But Deepanita was lost in her own world. Siddharth was still looking at her and was voicing something her heart refused to hear and understand.

Aparajita took charge again and addressed the principal, 'Okay we have taken enough of your time. Sir, please forgive us for this.' The principal sitting in the front row stood up, smiled kindly and said, 'Bravo my dears. I am proud of you both.'

Their dance was a huge hit with the audience and the students asking for a repeat performance till they complied. As soon as they finished, they were thronged by their juniors for autographs and congratulatory notes. The next performance had started. Aniket, aware that the girls were hungry took Aparajita and Deepanita for some snacks. The college canteen was filled with students and parents.

Someone called out to Aparajita. As she turned, she recognised the voice. 'That was a mighty speech,' said the voice. 'Oh, Siddharth. You?? How nice to see you here today. When

In Pursuit of Ecstasy • **233**

did you err...come out???' Aparajita asked her senior whom she considered her arch enemy once. 'Deep, see,' she turned to let Deepanita know and found her friend mumbling an excuse to no one in particular and moving away quickly. 'Hey what happened to her??' Aparajita asked Aniket. Aniket looked equally puzzled. 'Siddharth I think she still has some grudges against you,' Aparajita said. 'Yes I know. You both carry on. I will go and check on her,' saying this he went after Deepanita.

Aniket and Aparajita moved towards the counter to order their favourite coffee and *aloor* chop. 'She behaved strangely, know?' Aparajita asked Aniket taking their tray from the counter to look for a seat.

'I think I know why,' Aniket winked at her. 'She is in love with our giant hero here. And he too cares a lot about her.'

'Really??' Aparajita asked incredulously.

'Yes!! You blind woman! Just wait and watch,' he replied jovially.

'Wow! That would be lovely. We all can get engaged together,' Aparajita said excitedly, jumping the guns.

'Mmmm...No. I want us to get engaged as soon as possible,' Aniket protested. 'I cannot wait any longer. I want you to be mine officially.'

'What rubbish?' Aparajita answered shyly but loving the urgency in Aniket's voice.

'Deep...,' Siddharth called after her as she hurried away blindly. She did not want to face him. He was all she had disliked and had conveyed the same to him repeatedly, despite her own heart betraying her; she had insulted him several times. *Wasn't that enough for him? And why was he following her? And that look...and what was he trying to say today?* Deepanita's movement became slower as her jumbled-up thought hampered her speed.

'Wait, don't run away from me like this,' Siddharth, who had caught up with her, halted her on her tracks. 'I have been aching to tell you this for so long.'

'What the…?' she turned to him angrily, but could not continue.

'Deep I am completely and madly in love with you,' Siddharth said without hesitation.

'What??' she asked him stupidly, not wanting to understand the things he was saying.

'I love you stupid girl. I had fallen for you the day I saw you protecting your able friend so ferociously. Fallen for your warm smile which is permanently there on your lovely lips, except whenever you see me,' Siddharth said smiling and consequently looking even more handsome.

She began to protest but he halted her by putting his own fingers on her lips. 'Please let me say this. I have been thinking of this day for the past one year. And it was the only wish that made my life inside the prison feel like a beautiful dream,' he confessed as he implored her to understand.

'Deep I might have been the wrong kind of person you think of me to be. But I have changed now. Believe me, I love you and want you to marry me. I have wanted to ask you this question for a long time. But you always managed to run away. I think you knew then as you know now…that…you and I, we have something in between us. This pull can be nothing but love. But how much do you love me, I really do not know. But I promise to keep you very happy. Please, marry me Deep,' Siddharth implored again.

Deepanita was dumbstruck and dizzy with emotions she herself could not identify. So she kept silent. They stood like that for a long time neither saying anything nor moving.

Siddharth finally broke the silence. 'Okay take your time. I know I am rushing things, and all this is too sudden for you. But please, please, say "yes" only.' And saying that Siddharth kissed her lightly on her lips unmindful of the stares they both got and vanished.

Deepanita was still in a trance. She kept walking slowly towards where her parents were sitting and sat down beside them. She found them smiling at her. She smiled back. Her eyes once again looked at the receding figure of Siddharth.

June 2010

'Aupora, Deep, come down. The boys and their families are here already. Aniket is threatening he will go upstairs if you don't come down and Siddharth is already on his way up,' Aparajita's mother called out.

The girls had just finished putting final touches to their make-up. They had heard Aparajita's mother but did not move immediately. They looked at each other meaningfully, smiled and raised each other's hands in the air gesturing combined victory.

'We made it,' said Aparajita, smiling broadly, looking tall and elegant in her gold and yellow outfit. 'Yes, we did it,' responded Deepanita looking equally flushed with happiness in her moss green *lehenga choli*, looking as pretty as her friend. Both hugged each other and stood in each other's embrace for a while, feeling nostalgic and emotional.

Siddharth and Aniket were knocking impatiently outside their door. 'Open up you two or we will break the door…we swear,' threatened Siddharth. 'Or at least make a serious dent to it,' added a somewhat unsure Aniket.

The girls hearing this laughed out loud. Aparajita went to open the door. Aniket and Siddharth who were about to pound the door once again stopped midway. 'Okay…okay…enough you two. You should give us some time you know,' said a smiling Aparajita.

'Two girls getting ready for their own engagement – not easy,' Aparajita mocked the boys, who stood smiling back foolishly at her.

'You look out of this world. So very beautiful, I just can't wait anymore,' said Aniket looking boyish and naughty in his crème *sherwani*. Aparajita laughed a shy laugh and went crimson in the face.

'Okay you two carry on, and move from the doorway. I need to go and check on my sweetheart,' the impatient Siddharth grumbled at Aparajita who complied easily.

Deepanita hearing the urgency in Siddharth's voice from inside the room smiled to herself. Siddharth found her still smiling – the same warm smile he found irresistible. 'Deep, I am such an idiot,' he said as soon as he saw her standing so calmly and looking like the gentle fairy princess his grandmother used to tell stories about.

'Why?' Deepanita asked concerned.

'I mean, I had you there in front of me and yet I kept fighting myself. I wasted so much of time. I could have lost you,' his eyes displayed the mixed emotions he felt. 'But now we are together, isn't it? Deepanita smiled shyly, loving him with all his heart. She had been a fool too, fighting him and her own self too. Deep down, she had known for a while that though she had been attracted to Aniket it was really Siddharth whom she had fallen madly in love with. She was very happy for Aniket and Aparajita and had moved on.

'Yes we are and I hope you know I am head over heels in love with you,' Siddharth reaffirmed. '...You have made me the happiest person on earth by agreeing to marry me. But now let's not delay anymore.' He held her hands and pulled her towards him to give the long kiss he had been wanting to. He wanted to go on forever. But knew that would delay the matters, so sensibly he controlled himself. 'Later I can do what I desperately want to,' he consoled himself and that brought out a wicked smile on his lips.

They were about to call out to the other two who were also lost in each other when they heard the fast approaching footsteps.

All hurriedly huddled up together in front of the large bedroom mirror, to take a last glance at each other and then went down for their respective engagements with their 'once upon a time adversaries'.

www.ingramcontent.com/pod-product-compliance
Lightning Source LLC
Chambersburg PA
CBHW031311150426
43191CB00005B/171